Working-Class White

Working-Class White

*The Making and Unmaking
of Race Relations*

Monica McDermott

UNIVERSITY OF CALIFORNIA PRESS

Berkeley   Los Angeles   London

University of California Press, one of the most distinguished
university presses in the United States, enriches lives around
the world by advancing scholarship in the humanities, social
sciences, and natural sciences. Its activities are supported by
the UC Press Foundation and by philanthropic contributions
from individuals and institutions. For more information,
visit www.ucpress.edu.

University of California Press
Berkeley and Los Angeles, California

University of California Press, Ltd.
London, England

Library of Congress Cataloging-in-Publication Data

McDermott, Monica, 1971–
    Working-class white : the making and unmaking of race
relations / Monica McDermott.
        p.   cm.
    Includes bibliographical references and index.
    ISBN-13: 978-0-520-24808-3 (cloth : alk. paper);
    ISBN-10: 0-520-24808-2 (cloth : alk. paper)—
    ISBN-13: 978-0-520-24809-0 (pbk. : alk. paper);
    ISBN-10: 0-520-24809-0 (pbk. : alk. paper)
        1. Prejudices—United States—Case studies.
        2. Sociology, Urban—United States—Case studies.
        3. Participant observation.
        4. Whites—Race identity—Georgia—Atlanta.
        5. Whites—Race identity—Massachusetts—Boston.
        6. Working class—Georgia—Atlanta—Attitudes.
        7. Working class—Massachusetts—Boston—Attitudes.
        8. United States—Race relations—Case studies.
        9. Atlanta (Ga.)—Race relations.
        10. Boston (Mass.)—Race relations.   I. Title.
    E184.A1 M136 2006
    305.5'62'0973091734—dc22   2005023238

Manufactured in the United States of America
15   14   13   12   11   10   09   08   07   06
10   9   8   7   6   5   4   3   2   1

This book is printed on New Leaf EcoBook 60, containing
60% post-consumer waste, processed chlorine free; 30%
de-inked recycled fiber, elemental chlorine free; and 10%
FSC-certified virgin fiber, totally chlorine free. EcoBook 60
is acid-free and meets the minimum requirements of
ANSI/ASTM D5634-01 (Permanence of Paper).

CONTENTS

List of Tables

vii

Preface and Acknowledgments

ix

Introduction

1

Chapter 1. The Cities and the Sites: "The Crescent"
in Atlanta and "Greenfield" in Boston

19

Chapter 2. Experiences of White Racial Identity

38

Chapter 3. Situational Contexts and Perceptions
of Prejudice

59

Chapter 4. The Implications of Diversity
among Blacks for White Attitudes

79

Chapter 5. Race, Crime, and Violence
104

Chapter 6. Race, Gender, and Sexuality
130

Conclusion
148

Appendix 1. Cashiers, Neighbors, and Regular Customers
157

Appendix 2. Notes on Methodology
159

Notes
163

References
167

Index
187

TABLES

1. General Demographic Characteristics of Atlanta
   and Boston, 1990 and 2000   20

2. Birthplace of Non-Hispanic Whites Living in the Atlanta
   and Boston Metropolitan Statistical Areas, 1980–2000   22

3. Birthplace of Non-Hispanic Blacks Living in the Atlanta
   and Boston Metropolitan Statistical Areas, 1980–2000   23

4. First Ancestry Mentioned by Non-Hispanic Whites Living
   in the Atlanta and Boston Metropolitan Statistical Areas,
   1980–2000   24

5. First Ancestry Mentioned by Non-Hispanic Blacks Living
   in the Atlanta and Boston Metropolitan Statistical Areas,
   1980–2000   25

6. Racial Composition of the Population of Fulton County,
   Georgia, 2000   27

PREFACE AND
ACKNOWLEDGMENTS

My aim with this book is twofold. First, I provide empirical evidence of the continued existence of antiblack prejudice among white Americans, a prejudice that often coexists with friendliness, civility, and an avowed opposition to explicit racial discrimination. It is a prejudice that is contradictory and inconsistent, a "free-floating prejudice" that can be cued by situational and contextual factors. Second, I demonstrate the utility of a methodological approach little-used in sociology—targeted participant observation. The goal of targeted participant observation is to observe patterns of interaction and behavior by participating in an activity that is indirectly related to the phenomenon of interest. This method yields rich descriptions, not so much of the members of a community or an organization, as of specific social processes of interest that can be observed only while one actively participates in a community's daily life.

For a total of approximately one year, I worked as a convenience store clerk in Atlanta and in Boston. My observations while on the job and in the study communities centered on the content and character of interracial interactions and, in racially homogenous settings, on my coworkers' and others' discourses about race. The end result is an excavation of day-to-day race relations in two working-class urban communities in the late 1990s. My findings reveal some of the same complexities evident in survey data on racial attitudes (Krysan 2000), as few whites in either city espoused an explicit desire for a return to legalized segregation. Yet negative stereotypes toward blacks emerged in the context of specific situations—discussions of crime or sex, for example. While many of these situational contexts had consistent effects across the two cities, there were also notable differences between working-class whites in the two communities with regard to the meaning that whiteness conferred in the specific localities where I worked. Many of the whites in the area I studied in Atlanta—a majority-white working-class neighborhood embedded in the "black" side of town—experienced their whiteness as a mark of individual weakness or failure: a successful white person should live and work in more affluent, suburban areas. In Boston, whites expressed no ambivalence about their position in racial hierarchies; instead, they understood their whiteness as a mark of superiority and privilege.

The research method I employ is somewhat unorthodox. There are a number of workplace ethnographies in which the researcher became a full-time employee in order to study the labor process or organizational dynamics (e.g., Burawoy 1979; see Hodson 2001 for an exhaustive bibliography). In contrast, I worked full-time as a convenience store clerk *not* to study workplace dynamics per se but as a way of both gaining access to local networks and obtaining an unobtrusive position from which to observe interactions among both strangers (occasional customers) and friends (regular customers and workers).[1] The specific sites were carefully chosen, based on GIS mapping of U.S. census data, in order to maximize the likelihood of observing black-white contact. While I have identified social processes likely to operate in many neighborhoods and communities in the United States, this project comprises two case studies and should be evaluated in concert with other studies of race relations in contemporary urban America rather than as a definitive statement in and of itself.

My method is distinct from traditional participant observation research in that I make no attempt to profile a community or describe participants engaged in a specific shared activity; instead, I am intent on using the vantage point of the corner store to describe the ways in which race structures life in two white working-class areas. Had I intended to describe the ways in which gender, for example, structures life in these communities, the pages that follow would, in many places, read very differently. The questions that oriented my research involved the apparent paradox observed by many analysts of contemporary racial attitudes and black-white race relations—namely, incontrovertible evidence of a reduction in the endorsement of the genetic superiority of whites, coexisting with high levels of residential segregation and widespread opposition among whites to many policies designed to reduce racial inequality. I initially suspected that the growth of the black middle class could have been threatening to working-class whites, who would respond with attitudes and choices in defense of any race-based advantages they might have. However, I did not find this to be the case in either city I studied, as class distinctions among blacks were rarely made by the whites I observed; when they were, the black middle class was (verbally, at least) admired rather than reviled. Instead, a growing awareness of the impropriety of publicly endorsing antiblack sentiments, coupled with economic insecurity and status anxiety, resulted in environments where race was rarely ignored or forgotten yet just as rarely spoken of in mixed-race company.[2]

Most whites are aware that expressing antiblack prejudice in mixed-race company is, at the very least, bad manners. In Boston, though less so in Atlanta, this awareness entailed the impropriety not only of making antiblack comments in front of blacks but also of making them in front of whites whom one does not know well.[3] Had I not spent six months in a low-wage job in their neighborhood, I suspect that many of the working-class whites I grew to know in Boston would have been much less forthcoming about their attitudes toward blacks than they in fact were after I earned their respect and trust. It is this respect and trust that constitute both the central advantage and the lurking danger of this methodological approach. The inherent ethical dangers render this approach useful only in cases where significant social desirability effects have been documented, such as in the study of racial attitudes (Groves and Couper 1998). With such subject matter, this approach can serve to peel away the polite façade that often characterizes contemporary black-white relations and expose the affective, situational, contextual interplay of race and behavior in contemporary urban America.

I am deeply grateful to a number of people who have provided thoughtful feedback and helpful encouragement to me as I conducted this study and wrote up the results. As will become obvious, I am deeply indebted to the men and women who accepted me into their workplaces, homes, and lives during the course of my research. I am especially grateful to the managers of "General Fuel" and "Quickie Mart" for being willing to hire me in the first place.

This book is based on research originally conducted for my dissertation in the Department of Sociology at Harvard University, where I was guided by a wonderful committee of faculty: Mary C. Waters, Lawrence D. Bobo, Christopher Winship, and Katherine Newman. First and foremost, my graduate adviser, Mary Waters, provided steady guidance and no-nonsense advice that proved useful on many fronts. I will always marvel at my good fortune in having encountered someone of such character and intellect so early in my career. Larry Bobo has also been enormously helpful to me in the conduct of this research as well as in the process of transforming it from a dissertation to a book. He is a true role model. Chris Winship provided many excellent comments on initial drafts of this work, while encouraging me to follow the combination of qualitative and quantitative methods used in social research. Kathy Newman also provided extremely useful feedback and guidance for which I am most thankful. I also benefited intellectually from my encounters with many other faculty at Harvard, including Andy Andrews, Gwen Dordick, David Frank, Stan Lieberson, Peter Marsden, Orlando Patterson, Barbara Reskin, and Yasemin Soysal.

A number of my fellow graduate students provided helpful feedback and support during the conduct of the fieldwork on which this work is based, especially Irene Bloemraad, Susan Dumais, Devon Johnson, Ziad Munson, and Mario Small. I also received helpful comments and advice from Bayliss Camp, Gaby Gonzalez, Tomás Jimenez, Ezell Lundy, Omar McRoberts, Wendy Roth, and Celeste Watkins. I would also like to acknowledge the support of an Eliot Fellowship from Harvard University.

Many of my colleagues at Stanford University have been helpful during the process of writing this book, especially those involved with the interdisciplinary Center for Comparative Studies in Race and Ethnicity, including Michele Elam, Hazel Markus, Paula Moya, Cecilia Ridgeway, Matt Snipp, Claude Steele, Dorothy Steele, and Sylvia Yanigisako. Visiting Fellows Amanda Lewis and Tyrone Forman also provided helpful comments, as well as welcome camaraderie. Susan Olzak and Rebecca Sandefur have been especially generous of their time and feedback, having carefully read the entire manuscript twice. Thank you both!

Some of the remarkable students at Stanford who have taken the time to comment on parts of the manuscript include Maya Beasley, Tomoka Higuchi, Amina Jones, Tahu Kukutai, Laura Lopez-Sanders, Marcela Muñiz, Donielle Prince, Frank Samson, Alicia Simmons, and Victor Thompson. Hana Shepherd not only provided invaluable research assistance but also gave helpful feedback on much of the manuscript. I have also appreciated the helpfulness and professionalism of Naomi Schneider at the University of California Press.

Finally, my deepest gratitude to my partner, Becky Sandefur, for her patience and thoughtfulness throughout the entire process.

Introduction

The South has long been posited as the geographic center of antiblack racism in the United States. The reasons for this association are numerous: slavery, legally enforced racial segregation, political disenfranchisement, violence and turbulence during the civil rights movement, bitter school desegregation battles . . . the list goes on and on. At the same time, the South has also been the geographic center of black-white interaction, with court-mandated school desegregation and lower rates of residential racial segregation than seen in cities of the Northeast or Midwest, and the region has retained the largest share of the black population in the country. In the words of Bill Manney, a black Chicagoan who moved to Alabama, "In the South, they don't care how close you get, as long as you don't get too big. In the North, they don't care how big you get, as long as you don't get too close."[1] This perception is mirrored in the comments of "Clovis," a white man and native southerner in his seventies whom I spoke to in Atlanta in the late 1990s: "I've traveled the whole country, and blacks have it the worst in the Northeast, where there will be street wars if they try to move into a white neighborhood."

The paradox of the relative ease of interpersonal relationships coexisting with greater levels of reported antiblack prejudice persists in the

South to this day. In the pages that follow, I provide some insights into the reasons why, in the process uncovering some of the subtle, locally situated ways in which race and class identity and experiences shape racial attitudes and behavior. I spent approximately one year working in retail jobs, primarily as a convenience store clerk in two predominantly white working-class neighborhoods that bordered predominantly black working-class neighborhoods—about six months in Atlanta and five months in Boston. My work provided me with a wealth of opportunities to observe interracial interactions and gather information about the ways in which whites' interactions with blacks fail to reflect the racial attitudes whites express when in exclusively white company.

Although whites in both cities were extremely reluctant to express antiblack prejudice in front of blacks, all-white settings provided fertile ground for the articulation of racial stereotypes and antiblack opinions. However, the nature of these comments, as well as the number and level of tension of interracial interactions, differed markedly between my two research sites: whites in Atlanta were often friendly and easygoing in their interactions with blacks yet would sometimes express strongly negative attitudes toward blacks in all-white settings; whites in Boston were not so easygoing in their interactions with blacks, and their expressions of antiblack prejudice often took the form of concerns about neighborhood racial composition, affirmative action, and crime.

One of the major reasons for these disparities is the different meanings attached to *white* racial identity in the two communities. Whites in the Boston neighborhood often identified themselves as working-class or as a member of an ethnic group with European roots; for many of them, being white conferred certain entitlements to "their" neighborhoods, schools, or jobs. In the Atlanta neighborhood, whites did not have strong class or ethnic identities to draw upon; instead, "white" was their primary identity, and their residence in a working-class community situated near black neighborhoods conferred a sense of failure for having not lived up to the affluent, suburban, privileged connotations of whiteness. Black-white interactions were neither threatening nor foreign to whites in the

Atlanta neighborhood, because these whites did not feel the strong sense of entitlement and privilege that whiteness often connotes. At the same time, they had little sense of being the same status as blacks. The relatively low status experienced by working-class whites in the Atlanta neighborhood stemmed from larger racist assumptions about the kinds of neighborhoods and jobs that whites *should* have. Failing to meet these expectations was a source of anger and, in some cases, shame. The anger sometimes took the form of harsh criticism of blacks as a group.

The patterns I identify and analyze are based on thousands of naturalistic observations I made while conducting my research. The research sites—two convenience stores in urban working-class neighborhoods—allowed me to examine the ways in which race and class are experienced in an ostensibly mundane setting, providing a window into the ways in which race and class structure daily life in the country as a whole. Throughout the United States, the legacy of hundreds of years of racial discrimination and prejudice is evident in the attitudes, emotions, and behaviors that Americans exhibit as they go about their daily lives. Increasing rates of intermarriage and decreasing rates of residential segregation belie the magnitude of racial division in the contemporary United States, which is borne out in statistics on wealth, income, occupation, life expectancy, educational attainment, and a host of other socio-demographic indicators. Trends in racial attitudes reflect these contradictory developments in late-twentieth-century America: while there has been a sharp decrease in support for strict segregation between races, there has been consistently strong opposition among whites toward affirmative action programs, a persistent endorsement of negative stereotypes of blacks by whites, and a large gap between blacks and whites in the amount of racial discrimination they perceive (Bobo 2001).

With such conflicting attitudes and contradictory trends, it is difficult to predict the role of race in daily interactions. If, for instance, a white man thinks that it is fine for a white woman to marry a black man but believes that blacks tend to be violent or unintelligent, how will this white man interact with the blacks he encounters as he goes about his business?

Will he be friendly and polite, avoid contact, or speak with condescension? Will he express himself differently with his white neighbor or store clerk than with a white survey taker or a black coworker? With so many contradictions and such instability in racial attitudes, the environmental and situational contexts of interracial interaction become especially important in determining behavioral outcomes. However, studies of micro-level contextual effects are difficult to conduct outside of somewhat artificial laboratory settings—they involve analyzing slices of "real life" for clues about the manifestations of racial attitudes in routine interactions.

One of the greatest obstacles to understanding the ways that white Americans understand race and experience their racial identity is the politically charged nature of race in the United States. Meanings attached to racial identity are difficult for many to articulate, but their manifestations can have huge implications for relations between blacks and whites in everyday life. Therefore, the discovery of these meanings depends on observations in a natural setting over a substantial period of time. My job as a convenience store clerk provided me with both an opportunity to observe interactions between a large number of whites and blacks going about their daily business and entrée into a variety of social networks as I became close with fellow cashiers and regular customers. My job made it easy to be accepted as a peer by local working-class residents, few of whom felt the need to modify their speech or reactions on the basis of my being a researcher. Since most of the people I studied were not aware that I was studying them, I have made every effort to provide for their confidentiality in this book.[2] None of the actual names of people, neighborhoods, or stores are used, and some minor details have been changed to ensure confidentiality.

The white working class is in an especially important position with regard to race relations in the United States. Working-class whites, especially in the northeastern United States, often express hostile attitudes toward nonwhite groups (Lambert and Taylor 1988). Many of the violent conflicts between whites and nonwhites have taken place in working-class neighborhoods, both because of greater rates of white exposure to nonwhites in such neighborhoods and schools and because of greater competition for jobs and other material resources. With the decline of the manufacturing sector and the rise of the service sector at the end of the twentieth century and the opening of the twenty-first, economic competition between working-class whites and nonwhites has only increased. The relatively high wages and security of unionized factory jobs are relics of another era; employment options for those without a college degree are increasingly limited and poorly remunerated. Between 1979 and 1993, the real hourly wages of all white men declined by 6 percent, while the wages of white men with less than a high school degree declined by 23 percent (Henwood 1997). Whereas educational attainment was relatively unimportant in determining occupational wages in 1949, it was vitally important by 1989 (Massey and Hirst 1998). Because more-affluent whites can use their economic resources to buy their way into neighborhoods and schools with small black populations, the whites who are most likely to be interacting with blacks on a daily basis are those who are less wealthy.

RACIAL INEQUALITY

Day-to-day experiences of interracial interactions and beliefs about race are rooted in a structure of racial inequality that predates the origins of the country. While the abolition of slavery and the legal and social successes of the civil rights movement mark major turning points in U.S. race relations, the legacies of slavery and segregationist laws and practices continue to shape contemporary race relations. Even though increasing numbers of Hispanic and Asian immigrants have reshaped the American racial landscape, in many respects the black-white divide remains the sharpest and strongest (Murguia and Forman 2003). Segregation in every major arena of social life, from the workplace to the neighborhood to the family, has not only solidified racial difference but also led to radically different understandings of inequality across racial lines.

Residential segregation is perhaps the most persistent and obvious manifestation of the black-white racial divide in the United States. Throughout most of the twentieth century, blacks migrated out of the South and into northeastern and midwestern cities, where a combination of racially discriminatory housing policies and "white flight" generated unprecedented levels of racial residential segregation (Massey and Denton 1993). While discriminatory mortgage lending was outlawed in 1968, there is evidence that such practices persist today (Yinger 1995). Neighborhood preferences are also an important aspect of racial segregation, although blacks and whites have strongly divergent perceptions of the ideal racial composition for their neighborhood: blacks prefer integrated neighborhoods more than whites do (Farley, Fielding, and Krysan 1997). Even though rates of black-white residential segregation have decreased since 1980, blacks are still more likely than Asians or Hispanics to be segregated from whites, especially in metropolitan areas in the Northeast and Midwest (Logan, Stults, and Farley 2004).

Segregation in neighborhoods leads to a host of negative consequences, especially for blacks living in majority-black, impoverished areas of cities (W. Wilson 1987). Access to jobs, resources, and quality schools is profoundly influenced by residential location, with majority-black neighborhoods lagging behind majority-white areas in all of these dimensions (Charles 2003). There is also evidence that employers use neighborhood of residence as a proxy for race as a way of screening out certain job applicants (Kirschenman and Neckerman 1991). In addition, the exposure that racial groups have to each other in public settings is influenced by both residential segregation and the relative size of each racial group. The segregated social networks facilitated by racial isolation not only impede black socioeconomic progress (Ellen and Turner 1997; Kasinitz and Rosenberg 1996) but also contribute to racial myths and rumors that can spark conflict (Fine and Turner 2001).

Residential segregation and racial differences in home ownership underlie the significant racial difference in wealth in the United States. Blacks, on average, have one tenth the assets of whites (Oliver and

Shapiro 1997; Conley 1999), a large and persistent gap that reflects the long-term consequences of racial discrimination in housing, as home ownership has been the cornerstone of wealth accumulation for most Americans. While not as extreme as disparities in wealth, black-white income inequality is still very much evident (e.g., Jaret, Reid, and Adelman 2003). Although the racial gap in wages has been gradually decreasing since the 1960s, blacks still make only a fraction of the earnings of their white counterparts. Additional evidence suggests that the negative wage effects of gender segregation in occupations is exaggerated for African American women, whose wages are more depressed by working in a female-dominated occupation than are the wages of whites, Hispanics, or Asians (Cotter, Hermsen, and Vanneman 2003).

A gulf between blacks and whites in earnings and status persists even among the most advantaged groups (Cotton 1990). Black executives in major corporations are often shunted to the least prestigious and remunerative positions, such as management of affirmative action programs or departments of human resources (S. Collins 1997). Even those African Americans at the very tops of their professions are less likely than whites to receive broad recognition for their accomplishments, with the exception of athletes and entertainers (McDermott 2002). Racial discrimination is frequently experienced by affluent blacks (Feagin and Sikes 1994). Perhaps because of such persistent racial disparities despite high class status, middle-class blacks are one of the most politically liberal groups in America, standing in sharp contrast to their affluent white counterparts (Hochschild 1995).

The court-ordered desegregation of public schools in the 1960s and 1970s resulted in protests and disinvestment in public education in a number of majority-white areas. Particularly in northern cities, the fierce defense of neighborhoods and schools from racial integration led to a number of violent clashes (McGreevy 1996). Consequently, schooling remains a racially contested arena, reinforcing the distance between whites and blacks. Many affluent whites, educated in a racially homogenous environment, have little contact with nonwhites during childhood.

While interracial contact is not necessarily synonymous with racial harmony, a lack of contact affords no opportunities for stereotypes to be challenged or for commonalities of experience and outlook to be realized. However, the effects of school desegregation on black educational outcomes and racial attitudes are ambiguous (Eitle and Eitle 2003); some black leaders advocate a return to the racially segregated school system that predated *Brown v. Board of Education*. Their wish is in the process of being granted, as segregation in U.S. schools has been on the rise since the late 1980s (Orfield 2001), co-occurring with a widening black-white gap in rates of college completion since the early 1990s (Blank 2001).

Such educational disparities pale in comparison to racial differences in experiences with the criminal justice system. Blacks, especially men, are not only dramatically more likely to be imprisoned than whites but are also more likely to live in high-crime neighborhoods and to be victims of crime (Kennedy 2001). While lower-income areas tend to have higher crime rates, affluent black neighborhoods are as crime prone as are poor white neighborhoods (Alba, Logan, and Bellair 1994; Sampson and Wilson 1995). With an imprisonment rate that is more than eight times that for non-Hispanic whites, and almost three times greater than it was in 1980 (Blumstein 2001), blacks are disproportionately impacted by anticrime laws, especially antidrug policies. While ethnic whites were once disproportionately represented among the nation's prison population, their arrest and imprisonment rates have sharply decreased since the 1980s; similarly, white working-class southerners are less overrepresented in the criminal justice system than in the pre–civil rights era though still more likely to be in prison than white working-class northerners (Hawkins 2001).

As recently as fifty years ago, racial differences were assumed to be so natural as to remain often unquestioned; there has undeniably been significant progress since the era of segregated lunch counters, schools, and busses. Nonetheless, significant racial divisions remain, especially between white and black Americans. Even in the arena in which there has arguably been the most progress since the Jim Crow era—racial attitudes—significant numbers of white Americans are still willing to openly endorse negative stereotypes of blacks and to express a desire for social distance from them.

RACIAL PREJUDICE

On reviewing survey data on racial attitudes, one might conclude that the most racially liberal whites in the United States are highly educated young women living outside the South. While the findings are not entirely unambiguous, social class, especially as measured by education, and residence in the South are often accurate predictors of racial tolerance among survey respondents. Regional differences reflect the cultural differences between the South and residents of other parts of the country. Given the South's history of slavery, Jim Crow laws, and often contentious civil rights battles, it is little surprise that southerners are more likely to have racially intolerant attitudes than residents of other regions (Schuman et al. 1997). However, it is somewhat surprising that the gap in tolerance levels between the North and South has remained constant over time (Ellison and Musick 1993); even among younger cohorts, southerners are much more conservative on racial issues than are northerners (Steeh and Schuman 1992).[3]

Since migrants from the South are likely to change their beliefs about race when they settle in a new area (T. Wilson 1986), it is reasonable to suppose that factors inherent in the southern environment rather than in the psyche of the southern mind are responsible for influencing racial attitudes. One such factor is the racial composition of the population. Since the South has a much larger black population than other parts of the country, feelings of competition or threat from blacks may be more likely to be elicited in the South. An additional key difference between the South and the rest of the country is the predominance of fundamentalist religions. Fundamentalist beliefs are often associated with politically conservative positions that have been found to influence racial attitudes (e.g., Yancey 2003, 179). Even though regional differences do not disappear after controlling for religion, they are lessened (Ellison and Musick 1993). In addition, the greater proportion of the South's population that resides in rural areas has been thought to contribute to the region's distinctiveness, as urbanites tend to be more tolerant and liberal than the inhabitants of rural areas. Regional differences are in fact reduced when the percentage of the population that is rural is taken into account (Fossett and Kiecolt 1989), although the differences between Atlanta and Boston survey respondents indicate that the rural-urban divide is not the full story (O'Connor, Tilly, and Bobo 2001).

Social class, especially as measured by education, is an important predictor of racial attitudes. The image of the blue-collar racist made popular by the 1970s TV sit-com *All in the Family* has its counterpart in academic research. For example, Lipset (1959, 1981), in his work on the authoritarian personality of the working class, claims that members of the working class are more likely to be antidemocratic and express racial intolerance than members of the middle class. The possible reasons for this difference are numerous, including economic insecurity, child-rearing practices, and social networks. While Lipset's work is not without merit, more recent studies have painted a more complex picture of the relationship between social class and racial attitudes. For instance, Wellman's research ([1977] 1993) finds that working-class subjects are *less* likely to express racist attitudes; their resistance to black nationalist politics, for example, is rooted in self-interest rather than an expression of authoritarian intolerance. On the other hand, Bonacich (1972) posits that the white working class is likely the most racially prejudiced group due to their feelings of economic competition with blacks. Steeh and Schuman (1992) report contradictory results with regard to class effects: education has a positive effect on tolerance, while income has a negative effect. The same effects are found with regard to perceptions of racial competition from blacks (Bobo and Hutchings 1996). Whites with high incomes are especially likely to oppose means-tested welfare programs (Steeh and Schuman 1992). Bobo and Hutchings (1996) find that Los Angeles whites with only a high school education are more likely to perceive competition from blacks than either the highly educated or those who did not complete high school.

As economic opportunities for those without a college education began shrinking in the wake of a reduction in the size of the manufacturing sector, feelings of racial competition rooted in economic fears began to characterize the perceptions of the younger (male) members of the white working class (Pinderhughes 1993). Not only were racist fears revived, but the white youths interviewed by Pinderhughes felt that they were *disadvantaged* by their white skin. This represents a shift from the racist attitudes of earlier cohorts, which were rooted in a sense of superiority and a desire for distance. In fact, Steeh and Schuman (1992) find that young, male, working-class urbanites were among the few subgroups that actually became more conservative during the 1980s (361).

While researchers have attributed the higher levels of racial intolerance among the working class to perceptions of group threat (Bobo and Hutchings 1996), the question remains as to why blacks are perceived as the threatening group. For instance, it is often college-educated whites who "replace" the less educated as jobs become more technologically demanding, and it is often the decisions of upper-class whites that leads to plant closings and reduced job opportunities. Why, then, is the sense of threat not targeted at those in another class rather than at those in another race? Part of the answer may lie in the susceptibility of attitudes to the pronouncements of those in positions of authority (Weigel and Howes 1985); if the political agenda is constructed such that blacks are portrayed as gaining ground at the expense of whites or as menacing the safety of whites, blacks will be viewed as a threatening group. Jackman (1994) persuasively argues that outward hostility is not the only indication of severe conflict, as peaceable relations are a common feature of relationships between oppressors and oppressed. In fact, open conflict suggests that the power of the dominant group is in the process of being seriously questioned, if not threatened. While the overall racial hierarchy in the United States has been remarkably stable for several centuries, the legitimacy of such a hierarchy has been increasingly challenged, arguably providing a language for challenging other systems of inequality that are not rooted in racial differences.

One might expect white working-class attitudes to be especially influenced by rates of contact with blacks. Jackman and Crane (1986) find that the effects on white racial attitudes of having a black friend or acquaintance is contingent upon the social class of the black contact. Having a black friend of lower socioeconomic status (SES) than oneself has no effect on attitudes, while having a black friend from a higher SES has a strong influence on both attitudes and policy preferences (478). Depending on the number of opportunities for cross-class friendships, working-class whites are more likely to have their racial views influenced by interracial friendships than middle-class whites, since the former are more likely to have black friends with higher status than themselves than whites who are already high status.

Given that both region and social class have an impact on white racial attitudes, an ethnographic study of white working-class neighborhoods in a northern and a southern city can reveal some of the contextual effects generating the responses reported to survey takers from a population among the most likely to have regular interracial contact.

DESIGN OF THE STUDY

Between 1996 and 1998 I worked in two predominantly white working-class communities in Boston and Atlanta for a period of about a year (about six months in Atlanta and about five months in Boston). While both sites were chosen to facilitate regional comparisons, they will not necessarily be representative either of the country as a whole or of their entire regions. Based on demographic profiles in the 1990 U.S. census, I chose neighborhoods that were predominantly white, with a minority of residents holding college degrees or professional jobs. In addition, at least one of the neighboring communities needed to be predominantly black; I selected such neighborhoods because they were the most likely to provide numerous instances of interracial contact. I also avoided selecting neighborhoods that were high-poverty areas, since I focused on the attitudes of the working class rather than those of the poor. The two specific research sites I ended up selecting were matched as closely as possible according to their profiles in census data and are described in greater detail in chapter 1.

Throughout this book I pay special attention to variations in meaning and context, central concerns of an area of sociology called symbolic interactionism. "Human activity involves transactions of meaning" (Maines 2001, 3), and perhaps nowhere is this more evident with regard to race than in interracial interactions in public settings. Meaning and intent are constantly being deciphered by participants in interactions, often through the lens of locally situated stereotypes linking race, behavior, and action. Both the cultural context and the social structure contribute to the meanings attached to race (Blumer 1958), and these meanings are necessarily moving targets.

Social interactions often contain information about the structured patterns of everyday life; such micro-level phenomena can reflect macro-level structures that encourage or constrain certain kinds of behavior. Symbolic interactionists such as Herbert Blumer and Erving Goffman have outlined the many ways in which our daily patterns of life symbolize understandings of larger social structures. The "social act" is the primary focus of symbolic interactionists (Blumer 1969); variation in social acts across contexts illustrates the effect of structures and institutions on individual behavior (Ulmer and Wilson 2003), while the interactions themselves reinforce shared understandings, prejudices, and stereotypes.

Such a focus on micro-level processes does not imply a lack of concern with large, impersonal social structures and the ways in which they shape the meanings attached to race and class; rather, the observations of specific interactions are interpreted in light of the racial inequalities, images, and politics of the larger society. The specific interactions may be relatively unimportant in and of themselves, but systematic observations of day-to-day life are vital to highlighting the ways in which large-scale processes of inequality (such as discrimination, unequal educational opportunities, and unemployment) are experienced and understood. Variations in understanding across time, place, and situation produce the tensions and contradictions that generate conflict and, ultimately, change in these larger social structures.

Blumer's (1958) development of a symbolic interactionist theory of race relations has had a major impact on recent research on racial attitudes in the United States. His theory of racial prejudice as motivated by a sense of group position, rather than by any innate feelings of racial animosity, has been quite useful in understanding survey results that indicate a positive correlation between, for example, the size of the black population and the strength of white racial prejudice (Quillian 1996; Bobo 1999). Blumer also emphasizes the importance of considering the meaning attached to things as an important object of study (1969, 3). It is not enough simply to report that working-class whites in the South are likely to endorse negative stereotypes of blacks or oppose affirmative action policies; rather, it is important to understand the meanings attached not only to certain policies and stereotypes but also to the identity markers "working class," "white," and "southern." Whether one feels pride or shame, security or uncertainty about one's own social identities can aid in understanding the connections between race, class, attitudes, and ultimately, behavior.

Face-to-face interactions—or in the words of Goffman (1983), the "interaction order"—are analytically distinct and important social domains (2). Through intimate study of micro-level interactions, one can begin to appreciate the differences between interactions that are *situated* in a given set of social relations versus those that are *situational* (3). Situated interactions happen to occur within a given set of social relations but could just as easily occur outside of these relations, whereas situational interactions are social exchanges that are constitutive of and bound by a given set of social relations. For example, a request by a child to his or her mother for some candy was an interaction I observed in both research sites, but the interaction had little to do with the social setting: it could have taken place in any public place in any city in the presence of any number of observers, but happened to be situated in the particular stores I was working in. In contrast, the comment "I usually look like a white man," uttered by a white neighbor of mine in Atlanta on being introduced to me, is not merely situated but situational: this neighborhood in Atlanta is characterized by many interactions in which racial identity is asserted in relationship to certain cues and status markers (in this case, the presence of my high-status landlord). Such interactions could not happen simply anywhere but reflect a localized understanding of race and status. It is the situational interactions that are the key to understanding the ways in which race is experienced and understood by Americans in the mundane activities of their daily lives. Such situational interactions are described and analyzed in the pages that follow.

RACE, CLASS, AND THE BOUNDARIES OF THIS STUDY

Defining "race" and "class" is problematic even when referring to official statistics or scientifically collected survey data. When these social constructions are important variables in a qualitative study, their murkiness is even greater. For this reason, I want to be clear about the ways in which I operationalize race and especially class while in the field.

"Race" is an ambiguous concept. Race is socially constructed (e.g., Memmi 2000; Omi and Winant 1986), and the categories "white" and "black" have had very different meanings and have encompassed different sets of people throughout the history of the United States (Allen 1994; Roediger 1991). In the fieldwork undertaken as part of this research, the meanings of "black" and "white" constitute part of the research question. The ways in which members of the communities define race for themselves and apply it to others is a key component of racial attitudes. For this reason, I identify people I encountered during my participant observation research as "white" or "black" according to their treatment and/or identification as such by members of the surrounding community. In cases where such information was not available, I racially classify individuals according to the prevailing norms of the localities in which I did my research. If this classification seemed ambiguous to me in a particular case, I recorded the person as "appearing to be" either white or black. While this discussion may seem to belabor the point, I want to emphasize that I do not hold race to be a natural classification but view it as a social construction with extremely important material consequences for individuals. For the purpose of choosing research sites that are predominantly "white working class," the racial composition of an area was based on data collected by the Census Bureau in which respondents place themselves into racial categories.

Class membership is an even trickier designation. The many theoretical schemas of class range from numerous carefully defined categories to an assertion that there are no socially meaningful class distinctions in the United States. My understanding of class in the fieldwork setting reflects the notion of social class based on relations of exploitation; this understanding privileges occupation and authority in the workplace over variables such as income or class self-identification. In an exploitation-centered conceptualization of class, education is understood as an exploitative asset to the extent that it is used to secure employment that results in higher levels of authority and control (Wright 1985). Hence, someone working as a convenience store clerk with a college degree would be considered working-class, since the position of clerk does not require a college degree.

This study will focus primarily on black-white relations and the attitudes of whites toward blacks. While relations among whites, blacks, and other racial groups such as Latinos or Asians are an interesting and important area for research, they are beyond the scope of this study. In one of the fieldwork sites, the Asian population was tiny, and the Latino population, while growing, was also small and distant from the site. In some cases, comparisons between white attitudes toward blacks with white attitudes toward other minority groups might be appropriate, but an in-depth analysis of multiracial relationships would require numerous research sites and many years in the field.

PLAN OF THE BOOK

The following chapter provides an overview of the demographic history of the Atlanta and Boston regions as well as detailed descriptions of the research sites. Chapter 2 provides a discussion of the different meanings attached to being "white" in Atlanta and Boston. Even though the whites I observed and spoke with in both cities had virtually identical demographic profiles, their experiences of being white were very different, hinging in many ways on the very different character of the white working-class neighborhood in each area. Chapter 3 demonstrates some of the situational effects on whites' expression of prejudice. Relying on observations from the convenience stores in Atlanta and Boston, I isolated some of the characteristics of interactions and the settings in which they occur as being especially likely to hinder or facilitate overt expressions of prejudice. Chapter 4 examines the differing effects that the presence of phenotypically "black" immigrants—Africans in Atlanta and Haitians in Boston—has on the racial attitudes of native-born Americans. While native-born blacks in Atlanta are typically quite hostile toward African immigrants, their presence barely registers with native-born whites. Conversely, whites in Boston are very clear to distinguish Haitians from native-born blacks, singling out the Haitians for special animosity.

Chapters 5 and 6 discuss two themes of daily life in both neighborhoods that are intertwined with racial beliefs. Crime is a major factor in the lives of residents of both cities, whether white or black. In some cases fear of crime leads to the familiar demonization of black men, but there are a number of ways in which crime and race are less obviously connected, such as the intentional steering of whites away from poor black neighborhoods by blacks themselves or the heightened suspicion evoked by pairs of men of different races. The convenience store also proves to be an important locus for gender relations, as discussed in chapter 6. Race and gender have a long and complex interrelationship in the United States, and the legacies of subtle gender and race cues were enacted at the two stores where I worked. The book's conclusion brings together the diverse strands of the ethnographic observations to 1reassess the relationship between context and race, drawing a detailed picture of the lived reality of race in urban American at the close of the twenty-first century.

CHAPTER ONE

The Cities and the Sites

"The Crescent" in Atlanta and
"Greenfield" in Boston

In many respects, Atlanta and Boston are perfect opposites; Atlanta has a recent history of little overt racial conflict relative to the rest of the Deep South, while Boston's recent history involves a number of violent racial encounters. Boston has a long history as a port of call for immigrants to the United States, especially many European groups such as the Irish, Italians, and Portuguese. Atlanta has received comparatively little European immigration, as it was struggling to overcome the devastating effects of the Civil War while Boston underwent considerable industrial growth during the late nineteenth century. Consequently, identification with a European ancestry group is lower for whites in Atlanta than in Boston (according to the 2000 U.S. Census). In addition, blacks have always been a much larger proportion of Atlanta's population than of Boston's. Each city has also had a very different labor history, with Boston being a stronghold of labor unions while Atlanta's workers remained largely unorganized in a right-to-work state.[1]

The considerable differences in the demographics of the two metropolitan areas are evident in table 1. Blacks form a much larger percentage of the population in Atlanta than in Boston or the United States; within the city limits the percentage of Atlanta's residents who are black is more than double Boston's and about five times that for the United States.

Table 1. General Demographic Characteristics of Atlanta and Boston, 1990 and 2000

	White Population Percentage		Black Population Percentage		Median Family Income		Poverty Rate	
	1990	2000	1990	2000	1990	2000	1990	2000
City of Atlanta	31.1	33.4	67.1	61.2	$25,173	$37,231	27.3	24.4
Fulton County	47.8	48.1	49.9	44.6	$36,582	$58,143	18.4	15.7
Atlanta metropolitan statistical area	71.3	64.2	30.0	29.6	$41,618	$59,313	10.0	9.4
City of Boston	63.0	54.5	25.5	25.3	$34,377	$44,151	18.7	19.5
Suffolk County	66.1	57.8	22.5	22.2	$34,850	$44,361	18.1	19.0
Boston metropolitan statistical area	88.9	86.7	5.7	6.0	$48,618	$64,538	8.1	8.6
United States	80.3	75.1	12.1	12.3	$35,225	$50,046	13.7	12.4

Source: Data from 1990 and 2000 U.S. Census Summary File SF-1 and SF-3 files, analyzed by the author. Figures have been rounded and may not sum to 100 percent.

When comparing metropolitan areas, which include white and affluent suburban areas, the Boston area's black population is only 6 percent of the total, while blacks make up almost a third of the population of the metropolitan Atlanta area. While the contrast between median family incomes is not quite as stark, Boston is also a more affluent city than Atlanta.

While Boston has long served as a major destination for immigrants, much of Atlanta's growth has historically been fueled by internal migration, especially from the rural areas of the South. In recent years, Atlanta has become home to a significant number of African immigrants and to Mexican immigrants as well, although the Mexican American presence is less prominent in Atlanta than in other parts of the state. Boston has one of the largest concentrations of Caribbean immigrants in the country and has long been a bastion of white ethnic politics.

Table 2 shows the considerable differences in the regional origins of the non-Hispanic white population in the Atlanta and Boston metropolitan statistical areas (MSAs).[2] While Boston has a somewhat larger foreign-born population, the greatest difference is between the proportion of residents who were born in the region; three-quarters of white Boston residents were born in New England, while less than two-thirds of Atlanta's white population hails from the Deep South (the population of the Deep South states is almost twice that of the New England states). The long-term connection of many residents to the Boston area may, in part, explain the possessiveness that a number of whites display toward "their" neighborhoods and communities.

The foreign-born black population in both areas has increased dramatically in the last twenty years (table 3). While Boston has long been home to a vibrant West Indian community, the percentage of black residents who are foreign-born skyrocketed to 27 percent by 2000, driven largely by a huge influx of Haitians settling in the area. Atlanta's foreign-born black population has also increased considerably during the last twenty years, although it is still a relatively small proportion of the overall black population. In contrast to the white residents of the Atlanta

Table 2. *Birthplace of Non-Hispanic Whites Living in the Atlanta and Boston Metropolitan Statistical Areas, 1980–2000*

(*In percentages*)

	Atlanta		
Birthplace	*1980*	*1990*	*2000*
Foreign-born	2.4	3.0	3.6
Georgia	54.9	48.8	50.2
Deep South*	64.5	58.3	58.2
	Boston		
Birthplace	*1980*	*1990*	*2000*
Foreign-born	9.2	8.1	8.1
Massachusetts	74.0	71.1	70.4
New England**	78.5	75.6	75.6

Source: Data from U.S. Census 5 percent Integrated Public Use Microdata Sample (Ruggles et al. 2004), analyzed by the author.

*States of the Deep South include Alabama, Georgia, Louisiana, Mississippi, and South Carolina. Data from Georgia is included in Deep South percentages.

**New England includes Connecticut, Maine, Massachusetts, New Hampshire, Rhode Island, and Vermont. Data from Massachusetts is included in New England percentages.

MSA, a majority of the black population hails from the state of Georgia, although this proportion has been steadily declining.

The ethnic identity of whites and blacks in Atlanta and Boston is starkly different (see tables 4 and 5). Boston's reputation as an ethnically conscious city is borne out by census data: a majority of residents report an ethnic ancestry, including almost 25 percent Irish, 15 percent Italian, and 12 percent Haitian. In contrast, the ancestries identified by Atlanta residents reflect a relative lack of ethnic identity. For example, the most common ancestry claimed by whites in Atlanta is "American," and the most common among blacks is "Afro/African American."

Table 3. *Birthplace of Non-Hispanic Blacks Living in the Atlanta and Boston Metropolitan Statistical Areas, 1980–2000*

(In percentages)

	Atlanta		
Birthplace	*1980*	*1990*	*2000*
Foreign-born	1.1	2.7	5.9
Georgia	80.3	68.8	59.0
Deep South*	87.4	78.4	68.4
	Boston		
Birthplace	*1980*	*1990*	*2000*
Foreign-born	13.9	23.1	27.0
Massachusetts	50.4	47.1	50.3
New England**	51.5	48.1	51.2

Source: Data from U.S. Census 5 percent Integrated Public Use Microdata Sample (Ruggles et al.), analyzed by the author.

*States of the Deep South include Alabama, Georgia, Louisiana, Mississippi, and South Carolina. Data from Georgia is included in Deep South percentages.

**New England includes Connecticut, Maine, Massachusetts, New Hampshire, Rhode Island, and Vermont. Data from Massachusetts is included in New England percentages.

POLITICAL AND ECONOMIC HISTORY OF ATLANTA

In downtown Atlanta, a statue entitled "Phoenix Rising from the Ashes" symbolizes the city's comeback after near destruction by Sherman and his troops during the Civil War. Atlanta has rebuilt itself to become the largest and most influential city in the Deep South. Like many southern cities, Atlanta has always had a large black population. The black middle class has been both sizable in numbers and nationally prominent in influence. With four historically black colleges, including prestigious Spelman and Morehouse colleges, many of the black intellectual elite,

Table 4. *First Ancestry Mentioned by Non-Hispanic Whites Living in the Atlanta and Boston Metropolitan Statistical Areas, 1980–2000*

(In percentages)

	Atlanta			Boston		
Ancestry	*1980*	*1990*	*2000*	*1980*	*1990*	*2000*
American	10.3	10.8	16.7	3.6	2.8	4.2
Native American	1.9	2.4	0.8	0.2	0.2	0.1
English	32.3	17.2	10.9	13.0	10.4	8.4
French	2.4	2.7	1.7	4.9	3.5	3.2
French Canadian	0.2	0.4	0.5	1.1	2.6	2.8
German	9.9	16.8	9.1	3.9	6.4	4.1
Greek	0.3	0.4	0.4	1.6	1.4	1.3
Irish	11.1	13.4	9.1	25.8	26.2	23.0
Italian	1.4	2.6	3.4	15.1	15.8	15.4
Polish	1.1	1.7	1.5	3.1	3.1	2.8
Portuguese	0.1	0.1	0.1	1.6	1.6	2.2
Russian	0.7	1.0	0.7	3.0	3.0	2.2
Scotch Irish	*	4.6	2.5	*	1.8	1.6
Scottish	5.0	2.8	2.2	3.1	2.4	1.9
White/Caucasian	0.4	1.8	2.0	0.1	0.4	0.3
None reported	12.7	10.7	26.0	7.8	6.1	13.4

Source: Data from U.S. Census 5 percent Integrated Public Use Microdata Sample (Ruggles et al.), analyzed by the author.

*Not tabulated.

including E. Franklin Frazier and W. E. B. Du Bois, have lived and worked in Atlanta. As exemplified by Alonzo Herndon's Atlanta Life Insurance Company, Atlanta has long been home to successful black businesses. Today, the historically significant Sweet Auburn district and the Martin Luther King Jr. National Historical Site commemorate the rich legacy of black accomplishment in Atlanta, and one of Atlanta's selling points to potential tourists is its central place in black history.

Table 5. *First Ancestry Mentioned by Non-Hispanic Blacks Living in the Atlanta and Boston Metropolitan Statistical Areas, 1980–2000*

(In percentages)

	Atlanta			Boston		
Ancestry	*1980*	*1990*	*2000*	*1980*	*1990*	*2000*
African	0.8	*	2.9	2.1	*	4.3
African American	83.6	83.4	71.1	66.2	56.5	40.1
American	2.6	2.5	1.4	2.4	1.8	3.5
Barbadian	0	0.04	0.1	1.1	1.3	1.4
Black	*	*	3.8	*	*	4.1
Cape Verdean	0	0	0.02	0.6	1.6	2.4
Haitian	0	0.04	0.5	2.7	10.7	12.4
Jamaican	0.2	0.6	1.3	2.6	3.7	5.1
Trinidadian	0	0	0.2	0.9	1.1	1.6
West Indian	0.03	0	0.2	2.5	2.3	1.3
None reported	10.5	10.4	14.5	12.4	12.8	15.5

Source: Data from U.S. Census 5 percent Integrated Public Use Microdata Sample (Ruggles et al.), analyzed by the author.

*Not tabulated.

Although the black upper and middle classes have long thrived in Atlanta, they have coexisted alongside a large poor and working-class black population. Vast stretches of the city's southern half are populated by desperately poor black households; several notorious black housing projects have been leveled in recent years after their appalling conditions came under public scrutiny. Yet a number of large projects continue to populate the south side, as does mile after mile of small, rundown shacks. Interspersed among the poverty are solid working-class neighborhoods, a scattering of affluent black neighborhoods, and a small number of predominantly white neighborhoods. However, the vast majority of whites in Atlanta live in the northern half of the city.

The Atlanta metropolitan area is bisected by two major interstates: I-85 runs north to south and I-20 runs east to west. Most whites, and many affluent blacks, live in neighborhoods on the north side, while most blacks live south of I-20. Many of the suburban areas north of the city have higher property values and status than the middle-class suburbs to the south. Whites in the southern suburbs of Atlanta had a lower household income in 1989 than whites in either the northern suburbs or the city itself, the latter reflecting the concentration of urban whites in affluent north-side neighborhoods (Hartshorn and Ihlanfeldt 2000). Much of the "spatial mismatch" between low-wage laborers and available jobs in Atlanta reflects the concentration of less affluent blacks in the city and southern suburbs, where they are hampered by poor public transportation in getting to jobs generated in the northern suburbs (Ihlanfeldt and Sjoquist 2000). As a result, wages are often higher in the northern suburbs than in the city, especially for low-wage workers such as those in the fast-food industry (Ihlanfeldt and Young 1994).

The north-south division is manifested in violent crime rates, school quality, availability of jobs, and public perceptions of the desirability of residential neighborhoods. Atlanta's major industrial areas and its primary airport are located to the south of I-20, while its high-end shopping malls are located to the north. Atlanta's notorious traffic problems also reflect this divide, as commuters from the south rarely need contend with significant delays while those from the north are typically stranded in gridlock. Unlike many metropolitan areas, there is not a stark divide simply between the suburbs and the city, as northern parts of the City of Atlanta have experienced rapid job growth and have some of the highest real estate values of the entire region (Brookings Institution Center on Urban and Metropolitan Policy 2000).

This north-south divide is strongly associated with race (see table 6). Though Atlanta has been nicknamed "The City Too Busy to Hate," its history (and present) has been indelibly stamped by racial conflict, racialized politics, residential segregation, and patterns of economic development that have not benefited all races (or classes) equally. That said,

Table 6. *Racial Composition of the Population of Fulton County, Georgia, 2000*
(In percentages)

	White	Black	Asian
Central Atlanta	23.4	70.6	2.6
Northside	70.1	20.9	4.3
Southside	13.7	81.6	1.1

Calculated by the author from Atlanta Regional Commission compilation of U.S. Census data (www.atlreg.com).

Atlanta does have a favorable history when compared to cities like Birmingham and Little Rock, Boston or Chicago. The transition from the Jim Crow era proceeded with fewer incidents in Atlanta than in many other parts of the South, primarily due to a concerted effort by political and business leaders to avoid the negative economic impact that open racial conflict had in other cities (Bayor 2000).

Nonetheless, Atlanta is a highly segregated city. The dissimilarity index for the metropolitan area declined slightly between 1990 and 2000, from 65 to 63; much of the integration reflected in this figure is driven by suburban settlement patterns.[3] The segregation rate for the city itself is 80,[4] virtually unchanged from 1990. White-black segregation is highest among the most affluent households and lowest among poor households in the city. The Mumford Center for Comparative Urban Research found that the Atlanta metropolitan area had one of the highest rates of disparity between the central city and the suburbs, ranking 276th out of 326 metropolitan areas in the United States. For example, the unemployment rate in the city of Atlanta was 14 percent in 2000 (up from 9 percent in 1990) but only 4 percent in the suburbs (down from 4.6 percent in 1990).

Atlanta has never had a high level of unionization, instead employing a primarily low-wage, low-skilled labor force (Keating 2001). White labor unions have played a role in keeping black workers out of jobs as plumbers, electricians, and truck drivers (Bayor 2000), conspiring with employers to do so.

Such actions reflect a clear trumping of race-based over class-based interests. Aside from the notable Fulton Mills strike in 1914–15, the white workforce has been largely disorganized and quiescent.

The difference between Boston and Atlanta in the size of the black population is only one aspect of the different racial environments of the two cities. Atlanta is known as the "Black Mecca," attractive to middle-class blacks for the variety of social and employment opportunities in majority-black settings (Hewitt 2004). While majority-black jobs usually result in lower wages, Atlanta is one city in which this is not necessarily the case. Through black dominance of local government, majority-black jobs in construction and government have wages and benefits that are on par with those of majority-white jobs in the city (Hewitt 2004).

"The Crescent"

I call the specific neighborhood where I conducted research in Atlanta "the Crescent." The area comprises three census tracts, one primarily white and the other two predominantly black. The town I lived in, "Holton," is about 80 percent white and is bordered by predominantly black areas to the east and west (both areas are predominantly black and working class, with significant white populations). About 15 percent of all adults in Holton are college graduates; more than half the workforce is employed in blue-collar jobs. The biggest employer is retail trade, followed by clerical, skilled blue-collar, and service. The median family income is about $28,000, several thousand dollars below the national median, but only about a thousand dollars below the median for Atlanta as a whole. Less than 10 percent of the population of Holton lives in poverty, which is below the city average.

I made my initial visit to the Crescent during the summer of 1997 to find an apartment as well as to insure that the neighborhood resembled the area described by the 1990 census data. Beginning in August of 1997, I rented part of a duplex near the center of Holton. Most of my neighbors on the street were older whites who lived in small, well-tended single-family homes. A handful of the families on the street were younger black families with children, and there were younger white families with children who lived around the block, as well. I rarely saw most of my neighbors, with the exception of Jerry (who rented a nearby home) and Blanche (my next-door neighbor). The quality of the housing, based on external appearances, varied widely from block to block in Holton. The duplex I was renting was one of the most run-down homes on my street, and decrepit and boarded-up housing could be found on nearby streets. There were also well-maintained single-family homes scattered throughout Holton, as well as some multifamily housing in average condition.

"General Fuel"

Shortly after my arrival in Atlanta, I obtained a job as a clerk in "General Fuel," one of Atlanta's twenty-eight hundred convenience stores, and in an area department store. This work brought me into contact with a wide variety of people, many of whom were from the immediate area. Because the work did not demand constant activity, I found myself with plenty of time to talk with customers, who would often "hang out" for a while. I also formed close relationships with my coworkers, most of whom were black, which provided me with a window into black working-class racial attitudes as well as entrée into other social groups. Additionally, I developed friendships with a couple of regular customers (both whites), one of whom introduced me to a number of neighborhood residents.

I also spoke regularly with several people who lived on my street, all of whom were white. In addition, I became involved through one of my coworkers with a community organization, in which I met a number of people in the community (mainly black). However, the vast majority of my data came from my work in the convenience store. The store was extremely busy, and a wide range of people would come through on any given day; two registers were in operation at all times during the day shift, and only rarely did more than five minutes pass with no one in either line. While many of the customers were from the surrounding area, a number of other people would frequent the store due to its proximity to a major interstate and industrial area. These customers tended to be whites dressed in professional attire.

Aside from gasoline, the primary purchases were cigarettes, beer, soda, and snack food. The owner of the store preferred not to sell lottery tickets, as he was concerned about the types of people that might attract. A handful of personal items, such as toothpaste and hairbrushes, were sold at exorbitant prices and were only rarely purchased. There was also an automatic car wash available, although this was popular only with taxi cab drivers. One free weekly car wash was one of the "benefits" provided to General Fuel employees, along with unlimited coffee, fountain drinks, and popcorn.

The store was arranged with security the foremost consideration; four video cameras, with sound, ran constantly. The two cash registers were behind a wall of bullet-proof glass, as was the store safe and the supply of cigarettes. The entire parking area was well lit, and the store was extremely neat and well kept, both inside and out. Part of the reason the premises were so clean was the owner's practice of having more cashiers on duty than were actually needed to wait on customers. The extra cashier(s) could arrange shelves, clean, and watch customers to prevent shoplifting. I am certain the owner more than made up for his increased labor expense, as shoplifting was extremely rare, the store was not robbed once the entire time I was there, and customers would often extol the cleanliness of the restrooms. Employee morale was also quite high, given the nature of the job and the low wages. Each shift of cashiers would try to outdo the others by leaving the store cleaner than we had found it. In the words of several of my fellow cashiers on first shift, the store looked "pimp tight" after we finished our workday.

Most of my fellow cashiers were black, although there was one other white cashier who worked on my shift. In addition, most of the cashiers were women, although three were black men, and a white man did light maintenance at the store. Of the cashiers whom I worked with regularly, all but one had no plans to leave for other employment or schooling in the future. The owner was planning to retire and sell the business within the next five years, but the assistant manager and the day-shift cashiers were intent on staying at the store, which uncharacteristically gave automatic pay raises after every six months of employment. As a result, everyone who stopped working at General Fuel during my period of employment did so because they were fired. Vendors who regularly visited the store were mainly white men, although there was one black woman vendor. Hence, there were numerous interracial interactions within the store itself, as well as interactions between different social classes.

POLITICAL AND ECONOMIC
BACKGROUND OF BOSTON

In contrast to Atlanta's rise from the ashes of the Civil War, Boston has been a culturally and politically important city in America since the seventeenth century. Its location as a New England port has long rendered it an urban settlement for immigrants from Europe and elsewhere. The Boston metropolitan area is in many ways the antithesis of the urban sprawl that characterizes Atlanta and many other sunbelt cities—central-city Boston is still very much the commercial heart of the area, and while there are a number of corporate offices along suburban Route 128, Boston has nothing like the far-flung series of office complexes that dot the northern suburbs of Atlanta.

Nonetheless, the Boston metropolitan area, as well as the city itself, is highly racially segregated. While not divisible into a simple north-south dichotomy, many of Boston's black residents live in a handful of neighborhoods in the south-central section of the city, such as Roxbury, Mattapan, and parts of Dorchester. Reflecting the numerical concentration of whites in the Boston metropolitan area, many predominantly white neighborhoods of varying social-class compositions are located throughout the city itself as well as in the mainly white suburban areas.

Like many older cities of the Northeast and Midwest, Boston is a city of clearly demarcated neighborhoods, many with particular ethnic or cultural characteristics attached. South Boston, a low-income white neighborhood near the central business district, gained national notoriety during the early 1970s as a center of opposition to busing to achieve racial balance in the Boston Public Schools. Violent protests, with demonstrators often adopting overtly racist imagery, were nationally televised, cementing an association between Boston's white working class and racism in the minds of those whose knowledge of Boston was primarily through media representations. The reality, however, was not quite so simple; the issues surrounding the antibusing controversy involved more than antiblack racism (although there were plenty of racist sentiments expressed), if anything, demonstrating the hostile defense of neighborhood turf that threatened Bostonians could marshal in the face of externally imposed change (Formisano 1991). The anti-busing conflicts involved issues of elites versus nonelites, suburbs versus city, and paternalism versus independence as well as white versus black. White ethnic, often working-class "defended neighborhoods," in the words of Formisano (1991), were key to understanding both the antibusing conflicts of the 1970s and contemporary racial hostility. The sense of a clearly defined, autonomous, and relatively homogenous neighborhood can explain much of the defensiveness expressed by working-class Bostonians in the face of change. The movement of outsiders into a neighborhood or of outside influence into neighborhood institutions (such as schools) is experienced personally, much like a theft of or attack on something that is owned rather than jointly inhabited.

"Greenfield"

Boston contains fewer white working-class neighborhoods that are proximate to predominantly black neighborhoods than does Atlanta, chiefly because the black population is much smaller in Boston. However, one neighborhood, "Greenfield," is mainly white and mainly working-class (although there are middle-class pockets on its edges) and is located in a predominantly black corridor of the city. Greenfield is about two-thirds white. Unlike in similar areas of Atlanta, most of the whites in Greenfield identify with a traditional ethnic group, mainly Irish. In contrast, the most common ethnicity claimed by those in the Crescent is "American." An additional, potentially important difference between ethnic identifications in the two neighborhoods is the high percentage of blacks in Greenfield who identify as West Indian. While the majority of blacks in this part of Boston are native-born, a significant minority are either West Indian immigrants or claim West Indian heritage. Sixty percent of the workers in Greenfield are employed in white-collar jobs, most of them clerical positions; only 16 percent of adults aged twenty-five or older have received a bachelor's degree. Most adults are employed as clerical or service workers, and the median family income is about $34,000. This is slightly below the median family income for the city of Boston.

I tried, unsuccessfully, to find affordable rental housing in Greenfield and ended up commuting to my job from a neighborhood on the other side of the city.[5] In contrast to Holton, there was a shortage of available rental housing in Greenfield. The price of rental housing in the Boston metropolitan area is much higher than it is in the Atlanta metro area, and the vacancy rate is much lower. While all of the observations I recorded were from my time in the Greenfield neighborhood (*not* the neighborhood across town where I lived), the majority of these observations involve the convenience store, the neighboring bar, local stores, and a nearby bank. Occasionally I spent time in the homes of neighborhood residents, but most of the socializing with my coworkers and others I met in Greenfield took place in the store or at the bar.

"Quickie Mart"

The "Quickie Mart," the convenience store in Greenfield where I worked, was in the middle of a major commercial district of the neighborhood and was more commonly accessed by foot than by car.

Consequently, most of the customers were local residents rather than a mix of locals and outsiders. The presence of a lottery machine in the store insured a steady stream of regular customers, most of whom would stay in the store to scratch their tickets and fill out their bet slips. Both blacks and whites worked as vendors who visited the store regularly; all of the cashiers were white. In contrast to the store in Atlanta, my coworkers were all men when I first started work; a woman was hired about a month after I was. Both of the male cashiers had been working at the store for several years, and one of them had a second job as a bartender. The female cashier who was hired after I was had no other source of employment. As far as I knew, none of my coworkers viewed the job as short-term, and all of them were still working at the Quickie Mart when I left.

The store itself was run-down, and there would occasionally be graffiti painted near the front entrance, although the physical structure of the building was intact, with no broken windows and functioning locks on both external doors. The trash dumpster for the Quickie Mart was located in a dimly lit side alley, but otherwise the exterior of the store was well-lit with a fairly large (for Boston) parking area. While a video camera and VCR were prominently displayed by the cash register just inside the front entrance, the VCR contained no tape, so no store activity was actually recorded.[6] The Quickie Mart was open late, although not twenty-four hours a day, as was General Fuel. Consequently, the evening clerk was responsible for counting the money in the cash register drawer as well as taking inventory of the lottery tickets and moving them to a safe under the counter before closing for the night.

The Quickie Mart was larger than General Fuel in terms of square footage, but the overall number of customers was lower. In an average hour, roughly twenty-five customers would enter the store, including those who were simply purchasing lottery tickets. Milk was often on sale as a loss leader to entice customers into the store, and traffic would fluctuate somewhat relative to the price of milk at a nearby supermarket. The additional traffic from targeted milk purchasers did not typically have an impact on the number of observed interracial interactions, as these customers would often enter and exit the store quickly, as if on a mission. Although there was also a small section of fresh fruit and vegetables, much of the merchandise was typical convenience store fare, such as candy bars, soda, and cigarettes (but no beer, as the licensing fee to sell beer in Boston is prohibitive). A handful of white elderly customers would walk to the store from their homes and do all of their grocery shopping at the Quickie Mart, but most customers bought fewer than five items at a time. From early afternoon onward, many of the customers were adolescents from nearby schools buying snacks on their way home. A small group of white, black, and Hispanic boys in their early teens would congregate outside the front of the store until chased away by the store manager. Despite their relatively small number, they were an often exasperating presence and, I suspect, kept away customers who did not wish to run the gauntlet of taunts and spitballs to enter the store.

Across the street from the store was a bar that served as a social center for a number of neighborhood residents. Women composed about one-quarter of the regulars at the bar (one was also a bartender there), and most of the patrons were white. Many of the bar regulars were also recurrent customers at the convenience store. Virtually all of my close contacts in the Boston neighborhood were white; I spoke regularly with numerous black customers, but I was unable to form the close relationships with them that I formed with my black coworkers in Atlanta.

METHODS

My primary means of collecting data was by keeping a detailed log of each day's events and observations. In some situations it was possible to jot down notes on observations in a notebook as they occurred; however, this was typically too obtrusive. Stopping at the end of the day to record field notes, while not ideal, was usually the only available option. At the Boston site, I dictated my field notes into a digital recorder while driving home at the end of the day.[7] To protect the confidentiality of those I observed, no tape recordings were made nor pictures taken without express written consent from everyone involved. In addition, the actual names of the respondents are kept in an encoded and locked computer file, with only aliases reported in the field notes and subsequent reports on the research.[8]

Given the sensitive nature of racial attitudes, my intentions with regard to studying such attitudes were not announced to the subjects. I invoked a "cover story"; my stated intention was to conduct a study of the effects of economic restructuring on working people in the North and South. This subject is less charged than the subject of racial attitudes, yet it enabled me to ask questions of subjects that would seem odd if posed by someone who was not doing research. If I had stated my true research intentions at the outset, it would very likely have affected the validity of the data; in such cases, a certain amount of secrecy is therefore necessary (Mitchell 1993). The secrecy of the research grew less secure as my relationships with local residents became stronger; however, only one person guessed the true nature of my project. I informed those to whom I had grown closest of my actual research intentions before I left the sites.

While the research sites in the two cities were selected to be as similar as possible according to standard demographic data such as education, occupation, poverty rate, and racial composition, the divergent urban environments of Atlanta and Boston render each location qualitatively different. Some of the most important differences that might influence interracial interactions include the racial composition of the metropolitan area, the salience of European ethnic identities, the strength of labor unions and its attendant influence on working-class consciousness, the spatial organization of the cities, and the different histories of interracial interaction. The purpose of this research is not to determine which of these factors, if any, are of primary importance in framing contact between blacks and whites in the city—ultimately it would be impossible to specify causal primacy with only two in-depth case studies. Nonetheless, by observing thousands of interactions in natural settings in both locales, one may see the ways in which "contextual effects" such as differences in city demographics, history, and culture impact race relations in daily life.

The patterns of black-white interactions discussed in the chapters that follow were identified after a detailed coding of field notes when the entire period of research was completed. Some of the city differences, such as the influence of European ethnic identities and immigrant narratives, were immediately apparent shortly after beginning the second field study in Boston. Other disparities were evident only after months of analysis, such as the extent to which perceived slights motivated antiblack comments in the Crescent yet had little such effect in Greenfield. On many other dimensions, such as the associations between race, gender, and crime, urban context made little difference, as black men were stereotyped as more violent and prone to criminality than others in both the Crescent and Greenfield.

In both cities, race and place are undeniably interwoven. For affluent whites who commute from (or live and work in) distant suburbs, race may function more like an abstraction—a politically and socially important abstraction, but unlikely to be continually considered. For less affluent whites who live and work in close proximity to blacks, race is not a mere abstraction but a major factor in everyday life. In both the Crescent and Greenfield, schools, neighborhoods, jobs, sex, safety, shopping . . . all are subject to considerations of race. As a result, the impact of the substantially different urban environments of Atlanta and Boston can be recognized in the language and attitudes of working-class blacks and whites going about their daily lives. A history of neighborhood defense in Boston generates a very different posture toward black residential mobility than does a history of white flight fueled by rapid suburban growth in Atlanta; anger and aggression in Boston is countered by fatalism and frustration in Atlanta. Just as race itself is a complex social construction, so too are the contextual effects of urban environment on racial interactions a reflection of national, local, situational, and idiosyncratic factors that underlie social life in any American city.

CHAPTER TWO

Experiences of White Racial Identity

Light skin has always been synonymous with privilege and advantage in the United States, and with good reason. There continues to be a clear payoff, on average, for having white skin in terms of a host of socioeconomic and health-related measures. However, it is problematic to assume, as much of the literature on "whiteness" does, that having white skin automatically confers privileges and advantages not necessarily available to those with dark skin (Hartigan 1999). In past research, scholars have often set themselves the task of analyzing the historical moments in which the construction of "whiteness" occurred and the ways in which its legacy has persisted to the present time. However, whiteness does not function in an unambiguous fashion. In racially mixed working-class and poor areas, whiteness can serve as a hindrance as well as a mark of privilege. The extent to which whiteness can serve as a burden is conditioned by several factors: the labor market, the racial history of the neighborhood, and the level of class consciousness in the community.

In lower-income, racially mixed areas, white skin can serve as a liability in the job market, especially for low-skill jobs. An implicit assumption is that whites living or working in the area are damaged in some way; if they were "real" white people, they would have moved up and out by now. If one is white and seeking a low-wage job, the assumption is often that one has substance-abuse or other personal problems. Whites, according to this stereotype, should be at least middle-class and living in safe neighborhoods.

This perception about whites living in this type of neighborhood is held by most members of the community regardless of race or class. The stereotype's pervasiveness is one of the reasons that working-class whites respond so angrily to claims for equal opportunity or compensation for past discrimination on behalf of blacks. To these whites the payoff for light skin is not self-evident, and the racism they exhibit is of a defensive sort, as when a white person points to the similarities between blacks and whites, especially in terms of the difficulties they encounter in the world.

On the other hand, in a low-income, racially mixed area with a tight labor market and a history of working-class consciousness, whiteness is more likely to function as a mark of superiority than of inferiority. Social distancing and a dismissive air toward racial minorities on the part of whites are more typical of such an environment. White reactions to accusations of racism or prejudice are just as vociferous as in the neighborhood without the history of class consciousness, but whites are more likely to claim that blacks are less deserving because they haven't worked as hard, than that whites have suffered just as much as blacks and therefore neither group deserves any special treatment.

This is by no means to suggest that there is widespread "reverse discrimination" or even an end to white skin privilege. In the aggregate, whiteness pays big dividends. Whiteness as a perceived mark of inferiority is generated by the functioning of whiteness as a concomitant of privilege and benefit in the larger society. Identifying the situations where the association between whiteness and privilege does not hold informs our understanding of racial attitudes in two ways: the standard arguments in favor of programs to ameliorate the effects of antiblack prejudice will clash with the experience of a group of whites who are likely to have frequent interracial contact; and cases where whiteness does not confer privilege demonstrate the influence of neighborhood context, especially labor market conditions, on interactions between race and class.

The lack of a vocabulary for articulating inequality in anything other than a race-based language is the backdrop for the findings reported in this chapter. To the extent that low social status, blocked opportunity, decrepit housing, and failing schools are understood in terms of racial configurations and stereotypes rather than class-based, structured inequality, one can expect "whiteness" to be the touchstone for the articulation of the working-class white experience in neighborhoods like Greenfield and the Crescent.

WHITENESS AND INFERIORITY
IN THE CRESCENT, GEORGIA

The experience of whiteness in the Crescent provides an intriguing example of the ways in which racial cues are bound up with class and the local context. "White" is typically conceived in terms of economic and social advantage and residence in predominantly white, affluent areas. What, then, becomes of the white racial identity of those whites who are poor or working-class and live in an area with a substantial black, working-class population?

The results are not the standard ways in which whiteness typically functions in the United States—as invisible privilege, even for economically disadvantaged whites. Whiteness in this context does not simply function like "blackness" when the usual constellation of class and racial cues is reversed. Instead, whiteness becomes a badge of inferiority—one that is contingent upon a global view of whites as more deserving of nice neighborhoods and good jobs than blacks. It is also bound up with expectations about racial segregation and the characteristics of those who live in racially integrated areas.

Being a white person in this type of neighborhood is distinctly different from being a white person in a predominantly white area. The underlying assumption in the Crescent and Greenfield, held by both blacks and whites of various class backgrounds, was that the whites who lived and worked there were somehow defective; that the least capable whites were most likely to live among large numbers of poor and working-class blacks. As one of the black working-class men studied by Lamont (1999, 139) asserts, there "is no real reason for a white guy to be a failure."

Many whites in the area believed that systematic discrimination was being practiced against whites. Their belief was bolstered by generalizations—expressed by local blacks and whites—that whites in the Crescent were alcoholic, addicted to drugs, or mentally ill. I experienced this negative perception of whites shortly after beginning my stint as a cashier at General Fuel. After I had been working there for about two weeks, two black prostitutes who worked a corner near the store came in to buy some drinks and snack food. The store was busy, and I left my job stocking the soda cooler to help out the other cashier. The first customer I served was one of the prostitutes. When I told her the bill came to three dollars and some change, she told me that she already had given me a ten-dollar bill. When I told her that I hadn't received any money from her, she raised her voice, insisting that she had just laid it on the counter in front of me. The other four customers, all white men who were not regular customers (they did not seem to be from the neighborhood), looked around nervously. The other two cashiers, both black, stopped what they were doing and watched the scene unfold.

I restated that I hadn't taken the money. The prostitute yelled, "I saw you take it! I saw you take it and put it in your pocket!" I angrily denied taking the money and told her she could come back when the manager was around and watch the store's videotape. She yelled again that I had taken her money. I yelled back, "Pay your bill and get out of here or I'm going to call the cops!" She leaned through the window of the bullet-proof glass enclosure near my register and screamed, "Why you gonna call the cops? Did I curse at you? Did I?" One of the white men in line said, "I really think you should call the cops now." I leaned in toward the woman and shouted, "Get out of my face!" She backed away, cursing, as her partner paid her bill. As she was leaving, she shouted back, "You're not even worth it. A white person working in a place like this!"

This encounter reflects the attitudes toward working-class whites in the neighborhood. My white skin should have provided for a better job or employment in a better neighborhood. Instead, it served as a mark of inferiority, at least in the absence of other information about me.

The encounter also helped solidify my relationship with the other two cashiers who were working at the time, Madge and Telika. Madge is a black woman in her late twenties who had worked at General Fuel for more than a year; Telika is a black woman in her early twenties who had worked at the store since relocating from the Northeast a year before. At first, Telika muttered, "Girl, I can't believe you just did that." Then she said, "You can hang with me in my neighborhood anytime." Telika and Madge told the story to the next shift of cashiers (all black) who reacted with surprise to the story. One of the black women, Jamila (married and in her twenties), stared at me with her jaw open when she heard the story; she incredulously asked, "Did you really do that?" When I answered in the affirmative, she and the other cashiers began a session of raucous laughter, continuing to shake their heads in disbelief. The element of the situation that evoked the most surprise was not the scam the prostitute had attempted but my reaction to it—the expected behavior is to quietly accept the abuse. As I was later to learn, a dominant stereotype of whites in this area, held by blacks as well as many whites themselves, is that whites are weak and submissive.

The low number of readily available low-skill jobs coupled with the negative treatment received by many whites in the area supported a perception that whites were being discriminated against in the hiring process in favor of blacks. This perception was not the same as the oft repeated refrains against affirmative action in public discourse, which involve claims about preferential treatment, but instead involved the sense that an unspoken "whites need not apply" policy was in effect for low-skill jobs in the area. That whites in the Crescent were subject to such a judgment testifies to the powerful effect of racial and class segregation on the everyday expectations of Americans. While white skin privilege may have been turned on its head in this neighborhood, the negative stereotypes of poor and working-class whites who live among blacks have everything to do with the overarching racist paradigm governing urban America. Dead-end jobs, substandard housing, and high crime are associated with black neighborhoods and black people. While most Americans acknowledge the historical existence of blocked opportunities for blacks (especially in the Jim Crow South), an individualist worldview places much of the onus of success and failure on individual effort. This, in turn, often leads to cultural explanations of group disadvantage, the most familiar of which concern blacks and include the notions that inner-city blacks exhibit a culture of poverty, black men are violent, black women prefer to live off welfare, and so on. Structural explanations of disadvantage for whites or blacks are not a part of the standard American discourse (Bettie 2003). Whites in the Crescent present a case of positive group stereotypes serving as a hindrance to members of the dominant racial group, whose situation is more typical of members of a subordinate group. Cultural explanations based on group preferences fall apart, as whites are not typically thought to exhibit a culture of poverty or a proclivity for living off welfare. When cultural explanations are not available, the harshest of judgments about an individual ensue.

I discovered that simply having light skin guaranteed few of the privileges I had assumed it would as I attempted to secure employment in the neighborhood I had carefully chosen based on census tract data. I assumed that my background as a white, formerly working-class southerner would make access relatively easy. However, finding a low-paying, low-skill job in the Crescent is difficult regardless of one's race; hiring queues for jobs such as cashier or salesperson often consist of several dozen people (see Newman 1999 for a description of this situation in Harlem). Many of the stores with Help Wanted signs in the window were not currently hiring but liked to have a set of applications on file because of the high turnover rate in low-skilled jobs. Walk-in applications are especially unlikely to result in employment in relatively depressed neighborhoods in Atlanta (Finlay 2000), as a time lag of several months to more than a year between filing the application and being called for an interview is not uncommon.

A large retail store in Creekwood, a community near the Crescent, posted a hiring notice on the front door. When I inquired about the positions available, I was told to fill out an application the following Thursday at 3 P.M. When I arrived the next week, there were about twenty-five people lined up outside the personnel office, about 80 percent of whom were black, the rest white. The personnel manager arrived fifteen minutes late and allowed twelve people, including me, to come with her to the back office to fill out applications. She appeared to use two criteria in selecting prospective applicants: gender and appearance. Though about 20 percent of the applicant pool was male, all but one of those called to the back office were women. In addition, all of those selected were reasonably well dressed, but not overdressed (as were two of the female job seekers); we were wearing casual business attire rather than street clothes or our Sunday best. When we arrived in the back room, we were told that there were no full-time positions available, just one part-time position in the photography department. We were encouraged to fill out applications anyway in case an opening arose. In another case, a local grocery store had a three-week waiting list for an interview to be a cashier, with roughly fifteen interview slots available each week.

Given such stiff competition, my hopes of quickly finding a low-wage retail position began to dwindle after a week of avid searching. I tried different strategies—playing up my previous retail experience and playing down my educational background, for example—but the results were the same. Then I responded to an ad for a cashier at a gas station that was a five-minute drive from my house; I rushed over early in the morning on the day that the ad appeared and filled out an application. The store was small but clean, with a large enclosure of bulletproof glass surrounding two cash registers. A middle-aged black woman with large scars across her face cheerfully handed me the application form. This time I decided to be honest about my years of schooling, and I wrote a short essay about my academic interest in race relations and my desire to work in a racially diverse environment. I submitted the application to the usual refrain of "We'll call you if we need you," and left disappointed. However, the (white) owner of the store did call two hours later, quizzing me about my desire to work in a racially diverse location. Was I serious about the job? Did I know what kind of neighborhood this was? I managed to convince him of my willingness to work at General Fuel, and he told me to report for work at 6 A.M. the next day. He also mentioned that despite my being "overqualified" for the position, he would have to start me out at "$5.75 . . . just like everybody else. Then we can raise it up. But you have to start the same."

Clearly, I got this job in a way few residents of the Crescent could match. It was essentially an unsolicited writing sample that led to my being hired, a strategy not many applicants for this type of position would likely attempt, given their probable educational background and cultural experience. Even after getting the interview with the owner, I still needed to assure him that I knew what I would be getting into—that the racial composition of the store's workers and customers would not be an issue for me. It is difficult to determine whether it was my educational background, my race, or some other personal characteristic that led to such questioning. The fact that the owner's concern revolved around my adaptation to the racial composition of the workplace rather than its class composition, the hazardous nature of the workplace, or the repetitive and physically demanding qualities of some tasks required in the job suggests the salience of race in the labor market in this area. It is conceivable that employers' suspicions that white job applicants will not work well with black coworkers or customers made it difficult for low-skilled whites to obtain jobs in predominantly black areas. Only after I explicitly stated that I desired a "racially diverse" workplace did I obtain an interview for such a position.

After I had been working as a cashier at General Fuel for several days, a large, middle-aged white man in work clothes approached me. I was stocking sugar packets near the coffee machine and was out of earshot of the other (black) cashiers who were in the booth with the cash registers. The man leaned toward me and said, "It sure is good to see you working here." I thanked him and asked him if he came into the store a lot. He told me that he had just moved here and that he worked for "a wrecking company just up the street." I told him that I had also recently moved to Holton (the predominantly white part of the Crescent). He responded, "You know, a lot of white people have applied to work here, and they haven't hired any of them." His positive response to my working at General Fuel had less to do with my ability to efficiently stock sugar packets than with the group I represented, the stigmatized whites of Holton.

At this work site, community members' perceptions of antiwhite discrimination in employment are bolstered by white management's stated preferences for black employees. Hank, the white owner of the store, and Stephanie, the white manager, both of whom lived outside the city of Atlanta, later told me that they were leery of hiring whites from the neighborhood because they suspected most of them were drug abusers. One possible example of an avoidance of hiring white workers occurred after I had been working at the store for just over a month, when an opening arose on the second shift. A white man in his late fifties applied for the position; he'd spent years working as a gas station attendant at a store that had recently closed. I looked over his application and overheard his "interview" with Stephanie for a position as a clerk. He seemed to be ideal for the position from my perspective, with a clean record and no obvious signs of alcohol or drug addiction. However, Stephanie elected to leave the position unfilled rather than hire him. When I asked her why, she replied that "he just wasn't right" for the job. She refused to elaborate when I questioned her about it. While this is hardly sufficient proof of discrimination against a white job candidate, it is reasonable to surmise that either the man's age or his race had something to do with the decision not to hire him. Whatever the true reason for the rejection, such events fuel perceptions of discrimination against white job candidates in the area.

On another occasion, when Stephanie and I were the only cashiers on duty, she commented after a white male customer had left that "they're not used to seeing only white people in here." She told me that white men had worked in the store in the past, but they had been fired for one reason or another. I asked if there had ever been white women working in the store. "Sure," she responded and went on to talk about a white woman who had been employed about a year before. She was "funny" and "well liked," but she turned out to be a crack addict, although "she hid it really well." Stephanie and Hank didn't find out about the woman's crack habit until she started taking money from the cash register. Despite her addiction, her bottom teeth were not rotted away, which Stephanie said was the telltale sign of "being on the pipe."

Stephanie associated this incident with a general problem that whites in the area had with drugs. Conversely, black employees with drug problems were not viewed as representative of a widespread problem among neighborhood blacks. During the course of my employment at the store, two black employees (one male and one female, both in their early twenties) were fired for smoking marijuana while on the job; two more black employees were fired for theft. Hank's only comment about the drug incident involved bemoaning the fact that the male worker, Max, had been so reliable and he hated to lose Max over something so stupid. There were no recriminations over the hiring of black employees, no regret that one "should've known better" than to hire a black worker.

In an inversion of the typical scenario (e.g., S. Collins 1997), the negative behavior of one or two members of the local white population can be seen as representative of the group as a whole, while the negative behavior of black workers is seen as reflecting individual failings rather than behavior endemic to the entire group. Neighborhood residence and social class limit this projection of individual behavior on the group, as it was not believed that the entire white population of the United States, Georgia, or even Atlanta was seen as beset by drug problems. Rather, whites living in this specific section of Atlanta were viewed in this light. Both black and white residents of the Crescent held this perception.

Certainly there are numerous whites in the Crescent who are beset by drug and alcohol problems, mental illness, or substandard living conditions. On the other hand, a number of my neighbors in Holton did not fit the image of dysfunction projected on them. One wrote poetry, another did not touch alcohol or drugs for religious reasons, and a third had retired after thirty years with the same company. They were all painfully aware of the stereotypes about residents of Holton. They had stayed in Holton to be close to family members, friends, and churches. Among the older whites, the cost of housing pressured them to stay; proceeds from the sale of their homes would not have been enough to purchase a comparable home in the suburbs. In the words of one middle-aged white woman who lived in Holton, "It is one of the few places a person without a lot of money could live that wasn't either Section 8 or the projects."

In the Crescent, racial segregation, class inequality, and racial stereotypes create an atmosphere in which whiteness can signify individual failure. Employers often assume that a white person seeking a low-wage job in a racially mixed area must have substance-abuse or other personal problems. It is the flip side of the stereotype that blacks belong in service jobs or manual labor: whites should be at least middle-class and living in safe neighborhoods. In this way, the overarching racial paradigm in the United States facilitates the function of whiteness as a mark of inferiority; because white skin is associated with privilege and dark skin is not, whites who are not successful are subject to an especially low status.

The pervasiveness of the negative stereotypes of whites living in this type of neighborhood is one of the reasons that working-class whites in Atlanta are much less likely to perceive discrimination against blacks than are more affluent whites (Kluegel and Bobo 2001). The payoff for white skin is not evident to working-class whites, and their racist expressions are defensive; for instance, they point out that the difficulties blacks face in the world are no worse than their own.

This experience of white racial identity as stigma, while unusual, is not limited to inner-city Atlanta. The same complex relationship to whiteness is evident among poor whites who live near black neighborhoods in inner-city Detroit (Hartigan 1999). Known as "Hillbillies," these white descendents of migrants from Appalachia were "inscribed [with] a stigmatized intraracial distinction" based on a combination of their residence near inner-city blacks and their class position (18). The perceived stigma of being white also extends to a very different social group of multiracial young people. Some mixed-race women in the primarily white northwestern United States perceive the white parts of their identities as a stigma, and they consistently de-emphasize their whiteness as a way of creating for themselves a "meaningful" identity, distancing themselves from the legacy of oppression that they associate with white racial identity (Storrs 1999).

Whereas a vast array of local and situational factors can influence the meanings connected to whiteness for any individual, several factors stand out as being especially likely to facilitate a given understanding of white racial identity. The size of the local nonwhite population, the availability of other plausible racial identities from which to choose to affiliate, the social class of most whites in the local area, and the strength of white ethnic identities all encourage diverse understandings of what it means to be white. For whites living in the Crescent, an area with a large black population and many working-class or poor whites, the lack of a strong ethnic identification or other available racial identities will facilitate their experience of white racial identity as one of perceived stigma.

WHITENESS AND PRIVILEGE
IN GREENFIELD, MASSACHUSETTS

To the residents of Greenfield, white racial identity means something very different from the burden experienced by the residents of the Crescent. The behaviors and attitudes of the white working-class residents of

Greenfield are more in line with those presented in much of the extant literature on whiteness: whites often express a sense of superiority and an air of entitlement relative to blacks. At the same time, however, there is also a perception that the community is filled with whites that are damaged goods. For example, I was told by two of my white male coworkers that I would never find a "stable" man in Greenfield, that everyone was "messed up" in some way.

At the Quickie Mart in Greenfield there were numerous confrontations between cashiers and customers, but none that I either participated in or witnessed involved derision of race or status, though there were many interactions that involved racial stereotyping and accusations of prejudicial treatment. The objectively worse working conditions of the Quickie Mart—which was frequently dirty, disorganized, and permeated by a foul odor, yet paid the same hourly wage as the comparatively sparkling General Fuel—was hardly an elevation in status relative to the Atlanta store. However, no aspersions were cast on the clerks at the Quickie Mart for being white yet "working in place like this." Some conflicts at the Quickie Mart did involve accusations of racism—several of these incidents are detailed in chapter 3—but contact never involved asserting someone's worthlessness because he or she was white.

The low-wage labor market in the Boston area is quite different from that in Atlanta. While high-wage jobs are difficult to obtain for those without college educations (as is the case throughout the country), low-wage jobs are relatively plentiful in the Greenfield neighborhood. The Quickie Mart position was the first job that I applied for, and I was given the job on the spot after being grilled about my background. The manager, "Gus," is a white man in his fifties of Italian and Irish Catholic descent. One of the first questions he asked me after he received my job application was if I had any "street smarts." I replied that I did and assured him that I wasn't a "pinhead." Gus said that he didn't want me to "turn Harvard," meaning become fed up and quit, after a couple of weeks. I laughingly assured him that I would not. When I told him "the money would be nice, but I'm mainly doing it for the experience," he asked me if my "mommy was rich." I replied in the negative and said, "It isn't like that."

He noted approvingly that I had graduated from a Roman Catholic university with a large Irish and Italian Catholic student body and mentioned that he had gone to junior high in a predominantly Irish Catholic neighborhood and had taken courses at a Catholic college. He commented immediately after this that "we [the store employees] are like one family." He said he'd "give me a shot," finally admonishing me "not to be ashamed of my education."

After I had been working at the store for about three weeks, I was filling my coffee mug when Gus entered the store. I joked that I always "seemed to be doing nothing" when he arrived. He responded, "Hey, like I told you before, we're all family here; I don't care about none of that. I knew what I thought of you from the beginning." In marked contrast to my experience in Atlanta, where my task was to prove that I was a researcher unlike the other whites in the neighborhood, in Boston I had to prove that I was like the other "family" members I worked with—an impression that remained with the manager for at least several weeks after my hiring date.

Affirmative action was a fairly common topic of conversation at the bar across the street from the Quickie Mart. Racial hiring quotas, especially for the fire department and police force, were singled out for special condemnation. The white patrons of the bar voiced familiar arguments: that hiring should be based only on "merit," that affirmative action was inherently unfair, and that such policies did nothing to help relations between the races. This stands in contrast to discussions of affirmative action in Atlanta, of which I heard only two: one white man criticized the awarding of construction contracts to a black contractor, while a white police officer praised affirmative action policies and said they were "long overdue."

Independent of the discussion of any political issues regarding race, there was a clear desire to maintain social distance in many interactions between black and white strangers in the Boston store. As others have noted, there is considerably more friendly, informal contact between blacks and whites in the South (e.g., Edgar 1999) than in other regions. While I found this generalization to hold true in most circumstances, the social distancing in the Boston area had an additional component. The comportment of whites in encounters with black strangers in Greenfield was not only cool but also judgmental. The coolness is a hallmark of impersonal interactions in the Boston area regardless of the race of those involved, but an air of judgment held consistently in only two types of interactions: those between loud or unruly teenagers and older people (regardless of race), and those between blacks and whites.

For example, a black woman who appeared to be in her fifties or six-ties was waiting behind a white woman in her thirties who frequently came into the store with her young son. On this particular day, the boy had been playing with a toy while his mother waited, and after a couple of minutes had dropped the toy near the black woman's feet. This woman apparently did not realize that the toy belonged to the boy and asked me if I would like her to put the toy back where it belonged. As I replied that I would take care of it, the white woman angrily snapped, "That's his toy!" The black woman began apologizing profusely; the white woman merely stared straight ahead with a stony expression on her face. Moments later, the white woman rolled her eyes at me and ges-tured in the direction of the black woman. I interpreted the gesture as indicating not only disapproval but also dismissiveness, which she made with the assumption that I shared her perspective. The white woman was a regular customer who was typically polite and deferential toward my white coworkers and me.

Many whites in Greenfield expressed a clear desire to maintain phys-ical distance from blacks, both in neighborhoods and in schools. In a city that witnessed violent protests against mandatory school busing two decades before, it was perhaps not surprising to discover that whites in Greenfield were not happy about sending their children to predomi-nantly black schools. My white coworker Tonya arrived at work one morning furious that the school authorities assigned her child to a kindergarten in a predominantly black part of town. Since she was unable to find an open kindergarten slot in a different area, she kept her child out of school entirely.

Several residents of the area expressed concern about the increasing black presence in the neighborhood. One morning three older white women came into the otherwise empty store to buy lottery tickets. The three women had been harassed by several teenagers, some black and some white, who were hanging out in front of the store. One of the women, whom I recognized as a regular customer, expressed her indignation about the treatment that she and her friends had just been subjected to. We chatted a bit about how troublesome the young people were, and she leaned toward me, putting her elbows on the counter, and said, "You know, um, Greenfield's getting to be just as bad as Maxwell [a predominantly black neighborhood in Boston that had been predominantly white thirty years before] and Maxwell Avenue is awful." I nodded without saying anything in response. She replied, "You know, Greenfield used to not let blacks in at all, and now it's turning into Maxwell. It's awful." I made no response, and she quickly added that she lived on Central Avenue (in Greenfield) and that three families had moved in on her street (implying that the families were black) and that they were good people. "You know one of them was a teacher, another one was a lawn doctor [worked in landscaping], and they took care of their property," she said. "You know I think it's when they own their own property they're good, but when they're renters forget about it. They just don't care. They mess the place up, they wreck the places."

Several processes were at work in this exchange. One was the expression of a desire for physical distance from blacks similar to that expressed by Tonya with regard to the schooling of her child. A second was the quick and easy transition from speaking in terms of race to speaking in terms of class. Whiteness, in this example, is equated with upstanding behavior, home ownership, and stability. The woman found it necessary to point to the example of those blacks living on her street who embody the behaviors she had just ascribed to whites, quickly distancing herself from a purely racial argument to one that is based on class standing (home ownership versus renting). Also interesting is that she quickly moved from a race-based argument to a class-based one when I stopped nodding along with her story, possibly implying to her a tacit assumption that class prejudice is socially acceptable whereas racial prejudice is not.

The degree to which antiblack or pro-white sentiment is held in neighborhoods like Greenfield is likely underestimated in much survey research, as there is a clear understanding among residents that expressing such beliefs is not socially acceptable. One white woman in her fifties covered her mouth and said, "Oops!" after complaining about the influx of blacks into her neighborhood. Gus said about a former employee, "He was a good worker for a black; I mean, he was a good worker." And when a Haitian woman was having trouble using the store's copy machine, he said, "The instructions are right there in black and white English! I mean, the instructions are right there in black on the white piece of paper." When I directly asked Gus if he would answer my questions about race honestly if I were some surveyor whom he didn't know, he responded, "Sure I would. I'd tell you that I wasn't racist! I just don't like foreigners."

In Greenfield, white racial identity confers certain perceived rights and privileges: rights to white schools, white neighborhoods, and white jobs. While these expectations are largely invisible to middle- and upper-class whites, the working-class whites in Greenfield are constantly confronted with threats to their accustomed level of segregation and privilege. Daily interactions with blacks highlight the importance of certain privileges to this population, much as affirmative action programs adopted by colleges and universities have laid bare the privileged expectations of more affluent whites.

The experience of whiteness as privilege is by far the most common understanding of white racial identity in the United States. In some cases, simply identifying with whiteness is thought to yield a sense of superiority, which becomes a psychological advantage to those who are nonblack (Warren and Twine 1997). Studies of the working class in settings similar to the Greenfield neighborhood in Boston report similar findings. In neighborhoods with strong ethnic consciousness and high levels of unionization, working-class whites are likely to defend their turf and view themselves as morally superior to African Americans. Such patterns emerge in ethnographic and historical studies of working-class whites in Chicago (Suttles 1972; Hirsch 1995; Kefalas 2003), Detroit (Sugrue 1996), New Jersey (Lamont 2000), Baltimore (Durr 2003), Boston (Formisano 1991), and New York (Rieder 1985; Green, Strolovitch, and Wong 1998).

While the examples from Atlanta and Boston do not represent an exhaustive inventory of experiences of white racial identity, they nonetheless illustrate two fundamentally different ways of experiencing whiteness in the contemporary United States. Furthermore, each of these ways of experiencing white racial identity is more or less likely to occur given the existence of a constellation of social structural factors. Regardless of the experience of whiteness, each understanding of white racial identity stems from an overarching racial hierarchy in which whites are dominant and nonwhites are subordinate. White racial identity is a stigma for some whites a portion of the time, only because the expectations for whites—that they be materially advantaged and live apart from blacks—are not met.

White racial identity as an experience of privilege clearly corresponds, of course, with white dominance in the American racial landscape. Nonetheless, the privilege of whiteness can take several different forms, each emphasized by different literatures on the white racial experience. The defensive expression of white privilege is the form that has been the primary focus of past research. The working-class whites in Boston most clearly and consistently experience whiteness in this way— as a tenuous privilege that must be defended in neighborhoods, schools, and jobs. Other studies of the urban white working class reach similar conclusions. On the other hand, white racial identity is almost invisible to many whites, primarily those whose experience has afforded them little contact with but significant awareness of nonwhites. This experience of white privilege is also a dominant theme in the whiteness studies literature.

White racial identity is not fixed in an individual, but is instead experienced along a continuum of stigma and privilege. The two categories reflect different spatial arrangements; white racial identity experienced as stigma in one setting could be experienced as privilege in a different time and place. These differential experiences can exist within the same individual, subject to situational constraints in addition to spatial ones. For example, an individual might experience white racial identity as a stigmatized identity at the local level but as a privileged identity when the nation is the frame of reference (Delaney 2002).

It is not enough, however, to simply observe that group identities mean different things to different people at different times. It is crucial that types of white racial identity experience be specified, as each of these experiences have different implications for intergroup behavior and conflict. For example, when whiteness is experienced as privilege, conflict between white and nonwhite groups is likely to occur (Shanahan and Olzak 1999).

Despite similar socioeconomic backgrounds, whites in the Crescent in Atlanta and those in Greenfield in Boston have very different understandings of their own racial identities. It is likely that a combination of racial composition and the history of class and race relations contributes to these different perceptions. In Boston, blacks are a small percentage of the overall metropolitan population; their presence in the city's government and business elite has paled in comparison to their numerical, political, and economic strength in the Atlanta metropolitan area. Ethnic consciousness and conflict have also played a much larger role in Boston than in Atlanta. I observed only two occasions when whites in Atlanta referred to themselves as belonging to any ethnic group other than white; these both involved discussions of Cherokee heritage. Ethnic self-identification was much more frequent and fervent in Boston.

Additionally, working-class movements, especially labor unions, have had a dramatically larger presence in Boston. While racial conflicts have been a significant problem for both cities, class consciousness has been a prominent feature of Boston rather than Atlanta. Whites in Greenfield described with pride their childhoods in housing projects, the long, hard days their fathers worked, and the discrimination their parents suffered under "Yankee" business owners.[1] Conversely, whites in the Crescent typically avoided discussions of humble origins. "White trash" was a commonly heard epithet in Greenfield but was rarely used in the Crescent.

While the attitudes of many working-class whites in both Boston and Atlanta can be characterized as "racist" in some respects, the character and manifestations of these attitudes is quite different in the two areas. Paradoxically, the success of working-class (sometimes racially exclusive) movements coupled with the overwhelming white majority in the Boston area may have leant an air of superiority to the whites in Greenfield relative to blacks. In Boston, there are material gains to protect; in Atlanta, poor and working-class whites see less of the payoff of having white skin. This is somewhat ironic, as one of the central reasons that unions failed to make much headway in the South was the alliance between working-class whites and textile owners—if owners kept black workers out, whites would agree not to unionize (Miller 1980).

The research of Blumer (1958) and others suggests that a desire to protect resources secured through racial privilege is an important cause of racist attitudes. Whether accurate or not, the perception of most whites in the Crescent is that they have not reaped the benefits of whiteness, that white skin can actually be a liability. While certainly not free from racist attitudes, the expressions of racial animosity in the Crescent tend to be motivated more by defensiveness than by an assertion of rights or superiority. The paradoxical negative effects of being white in a poor neighborhood in a predominantly black city may be more frequently observed as increasing class polarization occurs in both the white and black communities. Hartigan (1999), for example, finds that many Detroit residents, both white and black, hold poor inner-city whites in low esteem. It is important to identify different experiences of white racial identity as a means of creating social and political interventions that appeal to the circumstances and understandings of different groups of whites. While historical narratives of the unique struggles (and successes) of African Americans might appeal to the sensibilities of whites who experience their racial identity as a privileged one, whites who experience their identity as a stigma are more likely to respond positively to an articulation of the similarities between class inequality and racial inequality.

In addition, considering white racial identity as neither a fixed, measurable construct nor a constantly shifting state of mind but as a set of patterned experiences can help in understanding the connections between identity and context. The two experiences of white racial identity described here can be thought to exist as "dynamic equilibria" (White 1992) resulting from processes of interaction and racial awareness that occur repeatedly in similar ways. Considering white racial identity as stigma or as privilege can be a first step in clarifying predictors of prejudice and racial conflict.

CHAPTER THREE

Situational Contexts and Perceptions of Prejudice

In both Greenfield in Boston and the Crescent in Atlanta, the overwhelming majority of interracial interactions were, if not cordial, unremarkable. This corresponds with research findings on customer-clerk interactions in New York and Philadelphia (Lee 2000, 2002). However, numerous interracial interactions in both locales *were* characterized by an attempt to decipher or hide racist intent. Working-class blacks were rarely certain if rude treatment was a result of their race or their class status. This uncertainty led them to be silent in the face of some racist actions, yet at other times they were vocal and accusatory in response to treatment that was simply rude without regard to race. In most cases, whites were very careful to censor their expressions of prejudiced attitudes when blacks were present. However, many whites who had perfectly cordial face-to-face interactions with blacks expressed prejudices once there were no blacks present. Blacks sometimes mistakenly accused whites of acting in a prejudicial manner, and whites would sometimes "slip" and make a racist comment in front of a black person; in these moments anger poured forth and overt conflict occurred.

Social psychologists who have studied the effects of perceived discrimination on the emotional well-being of black men have found that perceptions of racist intent can have powerful, long-lasting effects.

In one laboratory-based experiment, black men were asked to evaluate the extent to which a negative exchange they have with a store clerk (whose race is not specified) was racist; those men who viewed the exchange as racially motivated experienced more negative emotions than those who did not identify race as a factor (Bennett et al. 2004). Anger over the perceived racism of the exchange persisted even longer than did anger over a blatantly racist exchange between a white female store clerk and a black male customer (Bennett et al. 2004). Once emotional responses have emerged from an interaction, they can be "amplified" by continued interaction (Hallett 2003), and the attendant perceived discrimination can create bitter conflict.

Whites in both the Crescent and Greenfield very rarely expressed racial prejudice in multiracial settings, although such expressions were much more common when only whites were present. When no blacks were present, whites expressed antiblack sentiments in three main contexts: when the status of the white individual was challenged in some way; in reference to blacks' claims of discrimination; and in reference to neighborhood social problems, such as high crime rates or poor schools. The first context occurred most frequently in the Crescent, the second most frequently in Greenfield, and the third with roughly equal frequency in both areas. Since these conditions are rarely simulated in survey interviews, it is likely that survey data underestimate the extent to which whites harbor antiblack attitudes.

BLACK PERCEPTIONS OF WHITE PREJUDICE

Much of the information that I gathered on black perceptions of white prejudice emerged in the wake of exchanges between white customers and my black coworkers at General Fuel in the Crescent. In these exchanges, I was able to see what actually occurred and then hear how the black participant in the exchange interpreted it. Direct participant observation has an advantage over studies of black experiences of prejudice that rely solely on first-person accounts (e.g., Franklin 1991), because both sides of an exchange are observed. While I do not believe the black women whom I worked with were completely forthcoming about their attitudes toward whites in their initial conversations with me, they did gradually begin to complain more openly about the perceived racist behavior of customers and employers over time. Once I had been working at General Fuel for several months, comments of a derogatory nature about "white culture" were expressed with the introductory phrase "Don't take this wrong, but . . ."

Molina, a black woman in her late thirties with braided hair, a large tattoo on her arm, and sparkling gold-rimmed glasses, encountered numerous customers who treated her with disrespect. In one instance, she shoved an American Express card at me (I was working at the other register) and snapped at the customer, "She'll take you over here." The woman was in her thirties, well dressed, with blond hair and sunglasses, and appeared to be white and middle-class. I rang the woman up for her gas purchase with no problems. When she left the store, Molina said, "You know why I let you ring her up? She threw her credit card at me. Now I didn't see her throw nothin' at you now, did she?" I replied that she had not. "Now what is the only difference between me and you?" At this point she came up next to me, pulled our bare arms together, and said, "All right then!" When I asked her if this sort of thing happened a lot, she said, "Yeah! Don't you see it? They look at me, look at you, and then dip over into your line." I asked her what kinds of people did it; she replied, "Every kind."

Two factors were notable about these types of encounters: the white customers had no idea that their actions had affected Molina, much less that she had interpreted them as prejudiced; and the only information Molina used to reach her conclusions about the customers was that which was most salient to her—their race. There was no dialogue; while no racial slurs were uttered and the white participants were unlikely to have processed these events as acts of prejudice, such interactions exemplify the misunderstanding and hostility that can characterize black-white relations in the United States.

Molina's interpretation of the line-switching customers' actions as expressions of prejudice is at least partly correct; there was a clear preference expressed for my line by white, but not by black, customers. However, I also noticed that the only customers who did this were those dressed in business suits, clearly not from the neighborhood; I witnessed none of the locals switching lines. I was trying to get at this with my "what kinds of people switch lines" question, but Molina apparently did not make the connection that I did.

Another time, a white middle-aged man claimed to have given me a twenty-dollar bill, although he actually gave me a ten-dollar bill (this was a fairly common scheme). I eventually convinced him that he had, in fact, given me just ten dollars, and he stopped complaining and left. After he exited the store, Molina said, "You know that he would have been cursing *me* out for it. And you know why too, don't you?" She clearly meant that the man left quietly only because I was white. I suspected she was absolutely right in her suspicions; however, Molina did not witness the occasions when black customers played the twenty dollar–ten dollar switch with me and did *not* walk away calmly but created a commotion and demanded to see the manager.

There were also numerous black-white interactions with more overt expressions of contempt. For example, a well-dressed, older white man came into the store and was rung up by Molina. She asked him what the designs on his tie were. He responded with mock surprise: "You don't know what *these* are?!" He eventually told her that they were bridles. She said that she did not know anything about horses and could therefore not be expected to know that the designs were bridles. When he asked her what she thought they were, she smirked and responded, "Handcuffs!" The customer shook his head and muttered, "That's terrible." He asked her if she "knew about handcuffs." She said yes and nodded. He smiled at her and walked off. As he was almost out the door, she yelled, "My fiancé is really into them!" She started laughing and clapping her hands, exclaiming with glee that she "got him." She quickly became serious and asked me what he was thinking . . . she could not have a job "handling all this cash" if she had been convicted of a crime.

In this case, the white (seemingly middle-class) customer was attempting to make light conversation with Molina. In the process, he implicitly assumed that Molina had a criminal history, possibly because she was black. She picked up on this message and "got him" back with a clever comment. Her disgust was expressed *after* the customer left. He may have had a vague sense that he had expressed a racial stereotype, but did not see the extent to which Molina found this offensive.

This type of exchange happened with some regularity at General Fuel. Molina and Telika, a black woman in her twenties, both claimed there was no point in becoming angry with "rude" people. They would smile and act courteously toward difficult customers, then explode with anger as soon as the customer left. The most difficult customers were usually well-dressed whites; the black cashiers sometimes perceived their rudeness as racism, although they also witnessed the customers behaving with similar rudeness toward me.

I found it difficult to determine when customers were being rude because of racist beliefs or because such behavior typified all of their interactions—or because they were merely having a bad day. My presence at the other register provided something of a controlled experiment: if white people treated me with disdain, perhaps something other than race was involved. This was the logic that Telika, who had relocated from the Northeast a year before, used when a man threw his cash down rather than place it in my outstretched hand. After the man left the store, Telika exclaimed, "I hate it when they throw their money down like that. At least it's not because I'm black." Later that afternoon, she said that the weekly TV news show *20/20* should do a special on the way people act toward us (cashiers), "because they treat us like we're nothing." I agreed with her wholeheartedly.

At other times, black customers would interpret my actions as racist. This usually involved a quibble about the amount of money owed or the provision of a bag for a purchased soda or bag of chips.[1] In one instance, a black male customer became irate with me because I told him he would have to give me four dollars for four dollars' worth of gas (he'd given me only two dollars). He said, "Just give me four dollars' worth, *miss*. You're acting like I'm trying to rob the store or something."

In Greenfield, I asked a black male customer in his late twenties or early thirties if he would like a bag for his milk. This was my standard line for all customers who purchased large containers of milk, as a number of people preferred to carry the two-gallon jugs by the handle. In this instance, the man erupted, "Why are you asking me, miss? Of course I want a bag! Do you expect me to just carry this?!" He coldly stared at me, while I returned his stare and told him "it was just a question." As soon as he left, Gus, the white manager of the store, said, "You know what that was about, don't you?" I told him I suspected it was a racial thing. He replied, "You bet it is. It happens all the time."

A similar exchange occurred with Katoyah, a new employee at General Fuel. She was a large black woman in her twenties, with dreadlocks. When I asked Katoyah if she wanted to learn how to stock the cooler, the most arduous of the tasks at the store, she snapped back, "No, I don't want to do the cooler. What do you think I am, Samba Jane?" When I replied, "Excuse me?" she dropped her eyes, would not repeat what she said, and mumbled, "You must hate me."

At the Greenfield store, shoplifting was a serious problem. Local teenagers were the primary culprits, and we were instructed to closely watch anyone younger than twenty years of age who entered the store. While about half the young people were white, there were occasions when only blacks were in the store. This twice resulted in accusations of racism by customers, when in fact my coworkers and I were guilty of ageism, if anything.

These encounters point to the difficulty in determining the motivations behind rude or hostile treatment. In some instances, the motivating factor is no doubt racism; I know from my conversations with whites in the area that some of them hold deeply racist beliefs. And I witnessed Gus and

Tonya, my white female coworker in the Boston store, treat black immigrant customers differently from other customers. Nevertheless, not every act of rudeness is an act of prejudice, as the rude behavior of some white customers knew no racial boundaries. The high level of uncertainty about the meaning behind others' actions leads to much confusion and suspicion on the part of both whites and blacks.

In both the Crescent and Greenfield, blacks maintained an awareness that derogatory comments about whites were not to be uttered without apology or humor. While this awareness has been demonstrated among whites in a number of situations,[2] I noticed its operation among blacks in both areas.

In Greenfield, there were two occasions when young blacks apologized to whites for being "prejudiced" or "racist." Once, several adolescent black girls were browsing a rack at the front of the store near the cash register. I heard one of the girls exclaim loudly to another that she "talked like a white girl when you said" something about the "hairbrush." Although I had not been paying much attention to them or their conversation, I looked up at them after this comment. I saw the girl who had made it being nudged by one of her friends, who said, "Shhh!" and gestured in my direction. The girl who had spoken suddenly looked up at me with an embarrassed expression. I smiled and told her not to worry about it. She said, "I'm not a racist but it just slipped out." She and her friends chuckled to themselves and moved to another section of the store.

On the other occasion, an elderly white man named John was in line waiting to buy lottery tickets. He had been in line for quite some time behind a group of adolescent black boys who had finished their transactions but were lingering near the register. When one of the youths realized that John was waiting behind him, he quickly apologized, saying, "I'm sorry; I'm not prejudiced or nothin'." John replied that it was fine; he was retired and in no hurry. After the kids left, John looked puzzled and said to me: "That's the first time I've ever heard a black kid say he's not prejudiced!" I asked John why the kid had apologized to him, curious as to whether something had been said that I missed. John replied, "I dunno; must be something about black power."

John's comment was insightful, as the act of apologizing for prejudice or racism indicated a degree of power; in apologizing, one moves from the role of victim to that of perpetrator. By the same token, this might be part of the reason why whites accused of racism react so angrily—the power to act in a racist way and claim this behavior has been taken from them. In a sense, whites may be thinking, "If I want to be prejudiced, you'll know it—that was nothing."

INTERPERSONAL RELATIONSHIPS

In much of the South, interracial contact is frequent. Blacks and whites often shop at the same stores and malls, work together, attend school together, and live in proximate, if segregated, neighborhoods. Friendships were quite common between blacks and whites in the Crescent; there was an ease of conversation and a jocularity between blacks and whites there that was noticeably different from interracial contact in middle-class areas in the Northeast. However, in racially mixed, working-class Greenfield there was also considerable friendly interracial contact. Numerous interracial friendships existed, and several young interracial couples frequented the store. Nonetheless, a social distancing was evident in black-white interactions among strangers in Greenfield that was much less common in the Crescent.

Conversely, while waiting in the very long lines at a local grocery store in the Crescent, whites and blacks would routinely start conversations with one another. Even Jerry, my middle-aged white neighbor, who often made scathingly racist remarks, spoke fondly of the waitress that he enjoyed joking with at his daily hangout, the Breakfast Shop. He said she was the best waitress who worked there, "a black girl," and he always made sure he said something to her as soon as he entered the store each day. Many of the white patrons of General Fuel, especially the men, chatted and joked with the black female cashiers. Such conversations were typically bland and pleasant and rarely occurred with black male cashiers.

These congenial conversations did not necessarily reflect a lack of consciousness of racial differences, however. A middle-aged white male construction worker who spent a lot of time renovating apartments in an all-black housing project in Atlanta treated blacks congenially in face-to-face interactions, but was motivated to do so by racist assumptions. His advice for interacting with blacks living in the projects was, "You just have to know how to treat them. You go in there and act yourself. If it is your time to die, then it is your time to die." With the same spirit, Mike, a white barber, related an incident in which a black man peeked his head into the store and asked him if he cut "Afro-American hair." Mike said he responded, "I know of black American hair, but I don't know about no Afro-American hair." According to Mike, the black man laughed and asked him if he cut black American hair. Mike said he responded that he did not cut that, either, and the potential customer left. Mike thought the story very amusing.

Whites were not the only group to engage in stereotyping in the Crescent, as my black coworkers shared a number of their preconceptions about "white folks" with me. During the time I spent behind the counter at General Fuel, the tenor of the comments about white people and their behavior expressed by my black coworkers changed considerably. Initial comments about "white folks" centered on seemingly innocent questions embedded in stereotypes such as "Do Harvard boys really starch their shorts?" or "Why do white people take showers every day?"; gradually the remarks became sharper and more consistent statements of perception. Whites were viewed by the blacks I worked and socialized with as having two chief characteristics: weakness and affluence. The perception of affluence and privilege persisted despite the significant numbers of low-income whites in the area—these whites were typically not considered part of the larger group of "white people." This view was made clear to me only in the later stages of my fieldwork, when presumably less self-censoring was taking place among my colleagues.

CONTEXTS OF RACIAL ANIMOSITY

In the Crescent, racial stereotypes and negative comments about blacks were related to me with great frequency. Once I had been working at the Quickie Mart for several months, I was privy to a host of racist beliefs and comments in Greenfield as well. The vast majority of whites who expressed their disregard of blacks as a group were the same whites who laughed and joked with individual blacks on an almost daily basis.

While older white men spoke the most freely about their negative feelings about and perceptions of blacks, the white women I got to know fairly well held equally racist views (with one exception). One older white man spoke of "niggertown" (a predominantly black neighborhood) just before he told me how well different races got along in his neighborhood. Hostility toward blacks was expressed in three main contexts: when the status of the white individual was challenged in some way; in reference to blacks' claims of discrimination; and in reference to neighborhood social problems, such as high crime rates or poor schools.

The most vociferous expressions of hostility occurred in the second context. Claims by blacks that they had been discriminated against in some way were met with almost universal rage on the part of whites. Local civil rights leaders were often singled out for attack. The lone exception was a white police officer who felt that blacks are indeed being discriminated against in a variety of arenas and that affirmative action was necessary. This officer had grown up in the Northeast and was verbally harassed and physically attacked for being "a Yankee" when he first moved to Georgia to attend college in the early 1970s. He said he heard "nigger" used all the time, that it was part of the "whole mindset." "The good ol' boy system reigned" during the seventies, he said.

On several occasions, whites made negative comments about blacks in the first context—immediately after the whites had been embarrassed or criticized in some way. This type of reaction was illustrated the first day I moved to Holton when the landlord introduced me to one of my neighbors. The neighbor, a middle-aged, grizzled white man, was covered in engine grease; the landlord commented that he "usually didn't look quite so greasy." My neighbor immediately shot back, "No, I usually look like a white man," then shook my hand and introduced himself. Several days later, this neighbor was comparing our neighborhood with the "elite" (actually middle-class) part of Holton. He finished by stating that our part of town wasn't so bad but that rats have become a problem "because of the Cubans and Haitians" who had moved into Holton several years before. He claimed that the immigrants allowed their homes to deteriorate (he himself was living in an apartment that could easily have been condemned), but the city of Holton was "getting rid of the problem" by bulldozing their neighborhood. Indeed, several long streets on the other side of town are filled with boarded-up duplexes that once housed the immigrant population.

Earl, a white neighbor in his late fifties, expressed dismay at the cool reception he received at the hands of affluent blacks. According to him, blacks who have gotten their money since the civil rights movement treat "a white guy like, 'What the hell you doin' here, honky?' They're the problem." Earl's comments are all the more interesting in light of the role that race has played in his family. Earl's family no longer speaks to him because his daughter has had two children with a black man, and he has taken his daughter, her partner, and their children into his home. He said that he "like to have exploded" when he first discovered his daughter's pregnancy, but that "she is family, and that's all there is to it."

When I complained to another neighbor, Jerry, about the long lines at the nearest grocery store, he spat back, "There ain't nothing but blacks that shop there. I won't set foot in the place." Further discussion revealed the actual basis for his decision—the rude treatment he had received from two of the cashiers, one white and one black. In his mind, "I don't like to be treated rudely" had been translated into "I don't like to shop with blacks." Rather than conceptualize himself as the object of others' disrespect, Jerry would rather think of himself as a subject choosing to shop with certain kinds of people.

A similar thought process was followed by Harvey, a bedraggled white man in his fifties who did light maintenance and landscaping for General Fuel. We would often chat as he stood inside the store drinking a pint of milk during his break from yard work. One morning he pulled me outside the cage (the box of bulletproof glass containing the registers) and said, "My wife is in a nursing home." His wife was twenty years his senior and had appeared quite frail when I met her a few weeks earlier. I expressed my sympathies, and he started to shake his head, mumbling that it is "a lot of red tape, of paperwork." With a glance toward Telika in the cage, he lowered his voice and said, "Don't take me wrong, but the blacks get everything. All of my wife's Medicare is eaten up by the nursing home. Look in any grocery store, and you see women in heels, dressed really nicely, driving a new truck, and then they pay with food stamps except for $9. I have two old cars, a '77 and an '80 that I bought new. I bet they'll want me to get rid of one of them." Harvey was clearly upset about his wife's placement in a nursing home and was particularly bothered by his lack of financial resources for dealing with her health problems. His sense that "the system" had taken advantage of him was expressed in terms of blacks having taken advantage of the system. Rather than admit to needing more assistance, he castigated black women for using government aid to purchase luxury items. Later in the conversation, as Harvey was describing the nursing home ("clean but old"), he said that the black nurses there were "much better than the whites. They take much better care of her." As Harvey grew more distanced from the anger and humiliation he experienced with the financial aspects of the situation, he moved from describing blacks as freeloaders to blacks as skilled caretakers. After he said he had to get back to work, I asked him if there was anything I could do to help; he quickly shook his head, snapped "No," and walked away with a wave of his hand.

The second context facilitating the expression of racial hostility, blacks' assertions of racial discrimination, is evident in the comments of Sharon, a middle-aged white secretary at a police station. I had asked Sharon about some differences between the North and the South, and she had told me that white southerners had been taught to treat everyone equally, regardless of color. She launched into a long diatribe against blacks, "most of them from the North," who come down to Atlanta and claim that they are treated unfairly because of their race. She said the problem had gotten worse as more blacks had moved down from the North. Sharon cited two examples that demonstrated her point. First, a black police officer from the North had filed a complaint against a white officer who used "the 'N' word"; the white officer was suspended. The black officer, according to Sharon, claimed the white officer used "the 'N' word" because he knew the black officer would overhear him. Sharon was angered by this because she had heard the black officer who had filed the complaint use the "N" word when he spoke with other blacks, yet nothing had ever happened to him.

Second, Sharon related that a black prisoner had charged a white officer with police brutality. The prisoner was six foot four and 300 pounds, while the officer was five foot five and 130 pounds. According to Sharon, the prisoner's mother exclaimed, "You expect me to believe he beat you up?!" when she caught sight of the officer. After six witnesses to the incident were consulted, it became clear that the officer cuffed the black man after he struck his girlfriend in the face. The suspect claimed that the officer arrested him only because he was a black man hitting a "white bitch." Sharon repeated this part of the story several times, clearly upset by it. During the course of relating these incidents to me, Sharon paused to have friendly conversations with two black coworkers (one male and one female) who poked their heads into her office.

A similar sentiment was behind one of the (many) rebukes I got from Stephanie, the white assistant manager at General Fuel. While I was on break, a white man tried to pay for beer and gas he had already pumped with a credit card that was rejected. As he had no other form of payment, Stephanie called the police. By the time I arrived back in the store, five police officers were questioning the man. Despite his having no driver's license, no registration for his car, and no forms of identification, the police let him go without so much as a warning after he said he'd call his sister to pay for the gas. Later that day, I commented, in response to Telika's amazement that he wasn't given a ticket, that "white men can get away with anything. One can come into the store with an Uzi to rob us, and they'll just say, 'Sorry sir, you must be having a bad day.'" Stephanie quite angrily asked, "You know what you sound like?" I shot back, "No, what? What do I sound like?" She shook her head and said nothing. I interpreted her intended message as "Only blacks complain about racism," although her lack of response to my questions did not allow me to confirm this interpretation.

Hank, the owner of General Fuel, anticipated charges of racism from his black employees. One week, he went over every time card with a blue highlighter if it showed an employee had clocked in later than the time he or she was expected to be at work. In the case of my shift, this time had recently been changed from 6 A.M. to 5:45. I had clocked in between 5:46 and 5:49 A.M. each day and had a time card filled with blue ink. I complained loudly about this to Stephanie, who was in the cage with me at the time, forgetting that everything I said and did was being recorded by the store's surveillance system. Hank watched and heard the entire exchange on the video screen in the back office; he stepped out into the store and called me into his office. He asked, "What was the reaction to the time cards?" "Negative," I replied. He said that he did it just to get everyone's attention. "But *one* minute late?" I complained. He smiled and said it wasn't directed at me; he had to color mine because he would be accused of favoritism if he didn't, since I was white. He went on to say that it worked better than warning letters, which didn't work at all. I replied that "it would sure work for me." His response: "But you aren't like them." He went on to say that jobs are important to whites, but that an entire generation of blacks has been ruined by the welfare system. In Hank's case, his primary concern was to avoid charges of racism; he clearly felt that such charges would be without merit but that he must apply stricter standards to his white employees to avoid the accusation.

When Doug, a middle-aged white man who worked as a bus driver and was a daily customer at General Fuel, saw me reading a newspaper article about local political corruption involving a black councilwoman, he said, "They fight more among themselves. There is a lot more black against black than black against white. . . . See, that's what's wrong with the government." The notion that affluent blacks caused more harm to working-class and poor blacks than did whites was not unusual; affluent whites were almost never mentioned by either white or black working-class people. Doug did not deny the existence of white racism; when I once asked him if he thought there really were white racists, he replied, "Oh, sure there are." However, he did not connect white racism to blacks' complaints about unfair treatment. Policies designed to correct for the disadvantages caused by discrimination are viewed as unfair, especially toward "white southern men." Angry about recent charges of racism in a local police department, Doug said that "70 to 80 percent of the white Southern men I know have never said the word 'nigger' or 'spic' in their lives." He felt that people make unfair assumptions about white southern men, and he recalled tourists who "ask me to say 'y'all' because they think it's cute." For Doug, charges of white racism reflect stereotypes of the ignorant white southerner. Clovis's view that "blacks have it worst in the Northeast" was shared by others in the Crescent, fueling the resentment toward those who express derogatory stereotypes of southerners.

Several whites I spoke with thought that black leaders had taken advantage of "their own people" and that race was pushed as an issue so that a few powerful blacks could benefit from minority contracts, hiring quotas, and the like. Others complained about ministers and civil rights leaders taking money from their followers and using it to line their own pockets. In both scenarios, it is blacks that are responsible for their own fate; whites are absolved of any responsibility for blacks' socioeconomic problems. Older white men, in particular, decry the results of the civil rights movement (referred to simply as "civil rights"). None believe that Jim Crow laws were fair or necessary, but they view civil rights as having ushered in a wave of complaints and irresponsibility. For example, Earl thinks that race relations were much better in the Crescent during the sixties and seventies "because everyone knew their place." Younger blacks that came of age after civil rights "have a chip on their shoulder." Those aged thirty and up are all out working, while younger blacks are trying to "get what they can from the system."

An exception is Joyce, Doug's friend who works for a trucking company. She had recently written an article on white racism for a regional publication; in it, she described her experience growing up in the Appalachian Mountains. As she was telling me about it, Doug broke in and exclaimed that there wasn't any racism in the mountains because there weren't any blacks there. She exploded, "That's a myth! My great-great-great-grandfather had slaves. Six slaves. He had them chopping wood. Can you imagine giving someone that you own an ax?" She also described the bombing of her high school shortly after it had been integrated. Clearly, she is cognizant of the history of white racism and refuses to deny this history. However, when moving to a discussion of present-day Atlanta, Joyce repeated the familiar refrain of powerful blacks taking advantage of less powerful blacks. She described one leader's threats of filing a civil rights suit in order to secure the construction of electric and sewer lines across his property. Unlike most of the whites who criticized black leaders, however, Joyce was also critical of local white leaders.

Whites also express animosity toward blacks in the context of discussions of neighborhood problems, especially crime and poor schools. Disgust with the poor state of South Atlanta's public schools is widespread, among blacks as well as whites. Earl said, "The schools have gone from white to black, and I don't need to say anymore than that." While he knew that some blacks are well educated, have lots of money, and instill the "proper" values in their children, such as those who live in the Heights (an affluent black neighborhood in Atlanta), he believed that most blacks have none of these attributes.

Crime is a big issue in the Crescent, as I discuss further in chapter 4. Violence and theft are rampant. A police officer I spoke with admitted that the police could not control the problem and focused only on major crimes, which did *not* include most cases of assault. National chain stores were leaving the area because they were unable to prevent shoplifting and muggings in their parking lots. I had items stolen from me on more than one occasion, including the theft of my dog's leash and an air freshener from my truck. Guns were owned by most of the people that I worked with and were commonly displayed on the dashboards of cars. Shortly before I left the store, a man was shot and killed while he stopped at a pay phone outside a nearby convenience store.

While this atmosphere affected both black and white residents, there were certain racial overtones to the ways they conceptualized and dealt with crime. For example, both blacks and whites expressed the belief that white people are at greater risk for being a victim of crime in poor black neighborhoods. When asked for directions by white male customers, two of the black cashiers I worked with deliberately steered them away from a nearby neighborhood whose residents were black and poor.

In one predominantly black neighborhood in the Crescent, I drove slowly down a side street lined with duplexes in various states of disrepair. A group of about five black men were sitting outside one of the partially boarded-up buildings. As one of the men made eye contact with me, he leapt up from where he was sitting and began walking toward my truck, waving a packet of drugs back and forth. It was 2:30 in the afternoon. When I later expressed my surprise at the man's brazenness to Jan, a black cashier who had grown up in the neighborhood, she said he thought I wanted drugs because I was white. Doug shared Jan's opinion and castigated me for being in the neighborhood in the first place. He said he didn't ever want to hear of me driving in that part of town again, not even in the middle of the afternoon.

Doug's concern for my safety did not extend to my presence in equally drug-infested white neighborhoods. One evening he brought me to a party in one of these neighborhoods in Holton. A white man I had been speaking with became upset with Doug as we were talking and pulled a knife on Doug and held it to his throat. (The details of this incident are described in chapter 5.) Doug eventually talked his way out of the situation. When I later expressed my concern about this to Doug, he told me not to worry; he had "had it all under control."

As is common among other groups of whites, race and crime are strongly associated in the minds of the whites whom I encountered in the Crescent and in Greenfield. When Stephanie was giving me a list of places I could go at night by myself, she pointedly told me the neighborhoods were "mainly white." However, the oft described practices of whites crossing the street to avoid blacks, or women grasping their pocketbooks as a black man walks past, were not evident in the Crescent.

The disjunction between the reality of white violence and the perception of black threat was especially sharp in Greenfield. The majority of the fights, bottle tossings, knifings, and other assaults that I either witnessed or heard about involved only whites. However, I was warned about the "crews from the projects" and told not to approach suspicious black men in the store—to simply call the police.

At the Quickie Mart, the frozen-food section was looted by five men one evening when I was working alone; I dialed 911, but the men eluded the police. When Gus heard about it the following day, he asked me why I didn't stop them. I replied that there were too many of them, they were bigger than me, and I was scared. He asked, "Were they black?" I replied, "Yes." He nodded and told me I was right not to have intervened.

When I applied for the job as cashier at General Fuel in the Crescent, I told Hank, the owner, that I was a graduate student at Harvard studying race relations. After I had been working at the store for about a month and a half, he called me into his office. "'You studying race? Let me tell you about something racial. Lashawn [a black female cashier on third shift] has only been charging white people for beer. Two guys came up to the counter with twelve-packs of beer, and she only rang them up for a Sunday paper. Then a white guy came up with a single beer, and she charged him $1.25 [the correct price] for it. And Antoine [a male cashier on third shift] has been straight out stealing from people. He rings up a customer on the adding machine, signs out on the other register, gives them their change, and then pockets their money. I should have known better than to hire a man." Two interesting issues are presented in his descriptions of the thefts he witnessed on the videotape of the night shift. First, his "lesson" to me about race is, black people steal from white people. The white crack addict who had earlier taken money from the register was not accused of stealing because she was white, yet the black cashiers were framed as representatives of their race. The second issue is gender: a black *male* is the paradigmatic criminal in the eyes of Hank. When I asked him why he "should have known better than to hire a man," he said it's not that he *wouldn't* hire any, just that they are more likely to steal from him; he's always had more problems with men. He added that he would never hire anyone with a military background, since they always stole from him, as well.

Whites in Greenfield and the Crescent are more likely to express prejudice in certain situations than in others. Discussions of neighborhood problems, assaults on whites' self-esteem, and accusations of white discrimination made by blacks are especially likely to evoke racially prejudiced comments. In other situations, whites are unlikely to make prejudiced comments, but these three situations are quite common and, in most cases, difficult to avoid.

My research in two multiracial neighborhoods reveals how interpersonal interactions provide the foundation for perceptions of race and prejudice in the United States. The correspondence between prejudicial intent and the appearance of prejudice is far from perfect; in many cases, blacks fail to see the prejudice of whites, while in other cases blacks view white actions as prejudiced despite a lack of prejudicial intent. This lack of congruence leads not only to misperceptions among both groups about the existence of racism and racial differences but also to situations that are potentially explosive. White hostility is most overt in the face of accusations of prejudice that are believed to be false, and blacks who discover the "true" prejudicial beliefs of whites who appeared free of discriminatory behavior experience a heightened degree of suspicion of all whites. Repeated misperceived interactions solidify a gulf between the races that is difficult to breach.

Somewhat surprising is the development of a stance of "perpetrator of prejudice" on the part of some young blacks. Those blacks who apologize for acting in a prejudicial manner toward whites, whether their deeds are real or imagined, are momentarily taking on the power of actor rather than victim. The whites who receive such an apology are thrown off-guard—they react with surprise rather than anger. To the extent that both whites and blacks can be seen as more equal partners in daily interactions, the potential for conflict decreases.

Black attitudes can also influence white perceptions via intraracial conflict. When homogeneity of the racial category "black" is no longer taken for granted, this may have different possible effects on white attitudes toward the "blacks" whom whites encounter. They may either begin to question the validity of attaching any racial stereotype to blacks as a group, or grow even more comfortable in expressing racial stereotypes and slurs because they hear blacks making negative comments about each other. Some of these situations and responses are explored in the following chapter.

CHAPTER FOUR

The Implications of Diversity among Blacks for White Attitudes

In the past twenty-five years, considerable attention has been paid to diversity within the black community. While much previous scholarship often treated blacks as a homogenous group, work by scholars such as Hochschild (1995), Landry (1987), Dawson (1994), Dillingham (1981), and Feagin and Sikes (1994) has illustrated class divisions within the black community, especially highlighting the unique contradictions faced by the black middle class. In addition, waves of "black" immigrants from the West Indies in the past several decades have highlighted ethnic differences among blacks that are often manifested in hostile and conflictual ways (Kasinitz 1992; Waters 1999). What has remained relatively under-studied, however, is the implication of increasing diversity among blacks for the racial attitudes of whites. For example, do widening class divisions between blacks result in a different categorization of "blacks" for many whites, such that racial group membership is no longer the sole determinant of a racial attitude? Or do widening class divisions grant whites further permission to criticize government programs aimed at ameliorating racial differences in socioeconomic outcomes?

In many respects, the black working class is the forgotten group in discussions of black-white race relations (Kelley 1994). Poor blacks, especially those in the "underclass," have received the lion's share of attention; considerable research has also been devoted to the black middle class. However, if defined according to their occupations as reported in the U.S. census, the working class is over half of the American black population. Many of the same arguments Teixeira and Rogers (2000) make to support a reorientation of public opinion research toward the American working class, in general, can be applied to the black working class in particular. The working class not only is numerically dominant but also often provides swing votes in political contests. Furthermore, interactions between working-class blacks and working-class whites have laid the foundation for intense episodes of interracial conflict.

Expressions of admiration or hostility that working-class blacks make about poor blacks, middle-class blacks, and black immigrant groups can be overheard by whites in multiracial settings. It is reasonable to expect that these intraracial attitudes may influence white attitudes toward groups of blacks, possibly in ways that do not reflect the intentions of the speakers themselves. For example, several whites I spoke with in Atlanta who heard blacks themselves use the term "nigger" (in both friendly and derogatory contexts) could not understand the negative consequences of whites' usage of the term. In fact, the term "nigga" was used by many blacks as a friendly term for black men, not as an inflammatory racial slur. On the other hand, terms such as "nigger" and "ghetto" were sometimes used by working-class blacks as a means of drawing a boundary between themselves and poor blacks, with whom they were often confused by whites. These terms were assuredly not used by blacks as self-identifiers; however, whites who heard blacks use these terms categorized them as self-identifiers since they were accustomed to thinking of blacks as a homogenous, undifferentiated group.

Increasing ethnic and class diversity within the black community might be expected to decrease antiblack prejudice and the strength of negative stereotypes among whites. If whites see group differences among blacks, especially class differences, then stereotypes about the group as a whole could conceivably be more difficult to endorse. However, differentiation within the black community would have the opposite effect if blacks articulate differences but whites fail to see them. If, for instance, native-born blacks endorse negative stereotypes of black African immigrants while whites do not distinguish between black Africans and native-born blacks, the effect will be a reinforcement of white's negative stereotypes about all blacks. Whites can actually feel bolstered in their negative assessments of blacks by concluding that blacks themselves endorse their assessments.

The relative lack of attention paid to the black working class and the theoretical importance of interracial interactions within the working class are compelling reasons to assess black working-class attitudes toward whites. The attitudes of working-class blacks toward other blacks are important to investigate for two additional reasons: working-class blacks' verbal expressions of attitudes toward poor and middle-class blacks influence white perceptions of blacks as a group; and relationships between native-born blacks and black immigrants can influence relations between whites and native-born blacks.

AFRICAN IMMIGRANTS IN ATLANTA

Atlanta is a hub for African immigrants to the United States,[1] with most originating from the countries of Eritrea, Ethiopia, Ghana, Somalia, Liberia, and Nigeria (Bixler 1999). Estimates of the number of African immigrants currently in the Atlanta metro area range from 14,000 (Bixler 1999) to 85,000 (Roedemeier 2000). According to the 2000 census, 36,645 residents of the Atlanta MSA were born in Africa (J. Wilson 2003). According to a representative of an African immigrant association based in Atlanta, Africans are attracted to the area because of job opportunities and a perceived lack of discrimination in the job market (Roedemeier 2000). While Africans in the United States earn more than native-born blacks or West Indian immigrants, this advantage disappears when factors such as education, work experience, and English ability are accounted for (Dodoo 1997). In fact, Africans actually have a disadvantage in terms of returns to higher education (Dodoo 1997).

Relationships between African immigrants and native-born blacks have received infrequent attention from researchers, due no doubt to the relatively small numbers of African immigrants and the recency of this immigration. Arthur's 2000 monograph on African immigrants to the United States is entitled *Invisible Sojourners*, reflecting the absence of the group from much scholarly or public scrutiny. In contrast to the wealth of information about native-born black and West Indian immigrant relationships, there are no prominent case studies or interview data in the sociological literature on black–African immigrant relationships, although a survey of 650 African immigrants selected via a snowball sample was conducted in the 1990s (Arthur 2000). First-person accounts by African immigrants to the United States give some indication of Africans' attitudes toward native-born blacks, though it is skewed toward a middle-class perspective (Apraku 1996; Isaacs 1961); but there are no corresponding accounts from native-born blacks. Some of these first-person accounts reveal initial prejudices toward native-born blacks giving way to a shared sense of discrimination. For example, Apraku (1996) writes of the predominantly black high school that he attended: "Adams High School is, rather than Africa, the real jungle!" (100). He also claims that many Africans "are less aggressive and perhaps less emotional than black Americans" (114). However, after spending several months in Harlem, Apraku "could now relate to some of their frustrations, the broken dreams and hopes" (105). He ultimately concludes that he "was no more immune to racism or bigotry than any other black person in the United States" (105). On the other hand, Isaacs (1961, 135) thought that African students in the United States were "looked upon as barbarians or ex-barbarians who had become snobbish Europeans" (quoted in Apraku 1996, 113).

It is the latter perception that accords most closely with my observations of black American attitudes toward African immigrants in Atlanta. Virtually all of the interactions that I observed and comments I recorded took place at General Fuel in the Crescent. A large number of taxicab drivers would enter the store on a daily basis because of our proximity to a major interstate. The majority of these cab drivers were male African immigrants, distinguishable from native-born blacks by their dress and accented speech. All but one of the cabbies were men, and the lone woman was a native-born black. While the female cabbie was well liked by both the white and black workers at General Fuel, all of the interactions with the male African drivers were either overtly hostile or curt, gruff exchanges.[2] This held true for my interactions with the African cab drivers, as well, who resisted my attempts to engage them in conversation and were often rude as when they threw money down next to my outstretched hand.

African immigrant women tended to be concentrated in hair salons and nail parlors in a predominantly black neighborhood about five miles from General Fuel, bordering the Crescent. Working-class African immigrants are residentially concentrated in this same neighborhood. I never observed any African women in our store, and would have been unaware of their numerical presence in Atlanta had I not ventured into their neighborhood. Hence, all of my observations of native black–African immigrant interactions in Atlanta involve male immigrants. While I did observe native-born black men interacting with African immigrants, all of these encounters were unremarkable. The negative attitudes and anti-African stereotypes I overheard were expressed by black women to native-born blacks and whites (including me).

The first time I heard any negativity about Africans was prompted by a conversation with Madge about a famous black American actor. Madge, Telika, and I had been discussing movies, and none of us found this actor's latest performance deserving of praise. Madge launched into a diatribe against the actor, whom she initially referred to as "that colored guy"; she closed by stating that he must be African. She then threw out a stereotype of Africans that I was unfamiliar with but that would recur during my tenure at General Fuel. Africans, she said, "want their wives to keep popping out kids." Telika stared blankly at Madge, and I tried to maintain a nonchalant facade despite being taken off-guard by her comment. The conversation was interrupted at this point by our customer service duties, and I thought nothing more of the comment.

About two weeks later, however, an African cab driver paid Molina for gasoline and a car wash; while no niceties were exchanged, neither was the encounter explicitly hostile in any way. As soon as the cab driver was out the door, Molina blurted, "They be wanting their women to keep popping out kids; I ain't havin' no ten, twelve kids." Madge, who had made the similar comment two weeks earlier, replied, "That was in the old days." The phrasing and tenor of Molina's remark was curious, given that her contact with the African customer was in no way flirtatious nor was there any indication of a relationship other than clerk-customer. Molina's comment can be seen to reflect a desire to differentiate herself from African women along the lines of self-sufficiency and independence. Given the relative isolation of African immigrant women and their absence from jobs located outside their area of residence, it is probable that Molina (and others) infer that these women are under the control of their husbands. Since freedom, choice, and dignity were among the most closely held values for the female workers at General Fuel (possibly because their work lives rarely reflect these values), these became the points along which distinctions between them and other "blacks" were made.

Telika expressed a similar sentiment, albeit relating to choice of occupation rather than personal or sexual freedom. When she, Madge, and I were on duty behind the registers one afternoon, an African cab driver complained to us about the state of the men's restroom. Madge went to the back of the store to investigate and found nothing wrong with it; I double-checked, and it was indeed clean—some might say spotless, relative to the typical convenience store facilities. When we returned to the front of the store and re-entered the bulletproof cage surrounding the registers, Madge spat out, "Damn foreigners!" Neither of us reacted to her comment, but Telika wondered aloud about "why so many of them drive cabs. And like, all the people from ProPlus [a nearby cleaning service] look ghetto. And I know they must be making money.

It makes me scared to work there [at ProPlus]." The "ghetto" reference refers to blacks with speech patterns, styles, and mannerisms associated with poverty, especially in the projects. Earlier Telika, who was originally from New Jersey, had said to Madge, "I like Atlanta, but it's still like slavery down here," referring to the concentration of blacks in low-skill occupations. In these comments Telika differentiated herself and, by implication, the other cashiers at General Fuel from other groups of blacks—African immigrants and "ghetto" blacks. While the comments about the concentration of immigrants and "ghetto" blacks in certain occupations might appear innocuous, the fact that she made these comments in response to the objectionable behavior from the African cab driver, the condescending tone of her voice when she spoke, *and* her comment about being scared to work at ProPlus indicate derisiveness toward the other groups of blacks.

Telika's disdain for the African cab drivers became evident in another exchange she had with Madge. When an African cabbie who was a regular customer at General Fuel asked if we sold single AAA batteries, Telika reacted with indignation. She stared at the man, looked at the display of multipacks of batteries near the counter, and asked him why he would ask something like that. The man gave a dismissive wave of his hand, turned on his heel, and left the store. Telika snapped, "He should know we don't sell those." Madge and I were both chuckling over the excited state the typically unflappable Telika was in. Madge spouted her de rigueur comment after any African immigrants exited the store: "Damn foreigners!" Telika, still upset, responded, "He's not a foreigner; he comes in here all the time!" Telika meant not to chasten Madge for her comment about foreigners but rather to criticize the ignorance and rudeness of the customer. While reacting negatively to rude customers was hardly unusual, the intensity of Telika's response was indeed notable.

I observed one instance of a native-born black defending African immigrants, during a heated exchange between Telika and Madge. Madge had been the most consistent detractor of African customers, and her anger reached its zenith one afternoon in the face of a complaint

from an African man. While the three of us were behind the cash registers during an unseasonably cold day in November, the car wash located
behind the store stopped working shortly after an African taxi driver had
purchased a wash. The cabbie looked to be in his late forties, was very
thin, wore glasses, and was dressed in an inexpensive suit. When he
came into the store to complain about the car wash, Madge went out to
investigate the problem. After about fifteen minutes, she came back in
and was shivering, seemingly quite irritated. When the customers in the
store (both white and black) had left, she burst out, "Africans are so
rude!" Telika responded, "You don't mean Africans; you mean some
people." Madge insisted that she did, indeed, mean Africans, and said
that "they think they are better than us," they are so "high and mighty.
They don't realize they couldn't come over here if it weren't for us." In
the face of Telika's disapproving look and my (I hope) dispassionate
appearance, she clarified her meaning by going into more detail about
Africa. "It's a beautiful country," she said, and noted that there were
people in Africa who were quite wealthy. However, "just because you
[Africans] got to come to our country, it doesn't mean you are all that."
Telika only said, "Girl, he really made you mad, didn't he?"

Madge's comments about Africans—that they "think they are better
than us" and that "they couldn't have come over here if it weren't for
us"—resonate with African immigrants' perceptions of the attitudes
that native-born blacks hold about them. Apraku (1996), Arthur (2000),
and Weisbord (1974) report beliefs among African immigrants that they
are, in fact, superior to native-born blacks and that black Americans, in
turn, perceive this attitude. Arthur's study (2000) of African immigrants
echoes the findings of Stafford (1987), Waters (1999), and others with
regard to West Indian immigrants and perceptions of an advantage in
the labor market for foreign-born blacks; many accentuate their for-
eignness because they believe that it confers higher status. Native-born
blacks such as Madge chafe against rude treatment from African immigrants, interpreting this behavior as a reflection of the Africans' attempts at
asserting their superiority over her. While Telika also reacted negatively to

rude treatment from African customers, her negative reactions were triggered by African customers' behavior rather than by their mere presence. Since she and I were able to sip coffee in the warmth of the store while Madge spent fifteen minutes in frigid conditions attempting to placate the angry customer, it was easy for Telika to minimize the status threat posed by the African cabbie.

Other black female cashiers at General Fuel also expressed negative stereotypes of African immigrants. Tina, a twenty-three-year-old woman who began working at the store just a few weeks before my tenure ended, and Sheree, a young black cashier, were discussing their hairdresser's salon one afternoon in front of me and Stephanie, the white assistant manager. They were swapping stories about the "strange" practices of the hairdresser and others in the salon, who Sheree later identified as African. According to Tina, they were eating a raw, uncleaned fish (this elicited an expression of disgust from Stephanie); Sheree added, "They don't sit in chairs, just eat off the floor." While this information was relayed in a nonjudgmental tone of fascination with differing cultural practices, the tone changed when Tina began discussing the child-rearing practices of the people at the hair salon. She complained that they did not discipline their children, but "just let them run around wild." Tina described a time that she spanked her child in the salon and was chastised by the hairdresser for hitting children.[3] This reflects an interesting twist on the issue of child-rearing practices among West Indian immigrants reported by Waters (1999).[4] Her research indicates that native-born people often judge the immigrant group unfavorably for harsh child-rearing practices; in this case, Sheree and Tina looked down on the immigrant group for lax child-rearing practices.

Throughout the conversation, both Sheree and Tina referred to the hairdresser and her customers as "those people." When I asked what those people were, Sheree responded "Africans," with a tone that indicated that I should have known. Regardless of the veracity of the complaints about the women in the hair salon, Sheree and Tina—like Madge, Molina, and Telika—were clearly differentiating themselves from the immigrant group. In contrast to the comments of Madge, Molina, and Telika, however, I sensed that Stephanie and I were the intended audience of this practice of differentiation. While I hastily improvised a trip to the restroom to scribble furiously in my notebook, the effect on Stephanie appeared nonexistent. She never referred to African immigrants as anything other than "black" and never participated in conversations about them.

WEST INDIAN IMMIGRANTS IN BOSTON

My findings with regard to West Indian, primarily Haitian, immigrants in Boston are of a different character than my observations of African-black relationships in Atlanta. Since all of my coworkers in Boston were white, as were virtually all of my close contacts, I was not afforded much of a window into the attitudes of native-born blacks toward Haitians. The interactions between native-born black customers and Haitian customers that I did observe were all cold and unfriendly, with a handful of overtly hostile encounters. However, other immigrants who were regular customers in the store, primarily Jamaicans and Puerto Ricans, were friendly with both whites and native-born blacks.[5] Since the Haitians were singled out from other immigrants for negative treatment, it is not immigrant status per se that drove conflict between native born-whites and blacks on one hand and Haitians on the other. Instead, it is possible that both native-born blacks and whites in Greenfield experienced a sense of group threat from recent waves of Haitian immigration.

The first overt conflict I observed between a Haitian and native-born blacks occurred after I had been working at the Quickie Mart for just over a week. An altercation between a Haitian man and a native-born black couple occurred in the parking lot; I was unable to see what happened from behind the cash register, but the Haitian man entered the store gesticulating angrily at the couple. He looked at me and yelled, "They tried to run me down with their car!" I stared at him, as did the white female customer I had been ringing up. He mumbled, "Ignorant black folks." The white customer looked at me with raised eyebrows and then quickly exited the store. A few minutes later, the Haitian man passed the couple in the doorway of the store, and the black man stared at the Haitian. He started talking to his female companion about the violent things he would like to do to the Haitian. She glanced up at me, then said quietly to the man, "Not in the store." She smiled at me, and said, "You'd think he [the Haitian man] would have enough sense not to walk behind a car that is in reverse." The Haitian man's racial hostility in this exchange, from what I could hear, was directed at the native-born blacks, as the man's anger melded into the insult "ignorant black folks." While the black woman may have been encouraging her partner to curb his tongue because I was white, I have no evidence for this; however, neither one of them disparaged the Haitian man for being "Haitian" (or black, for that matter). As with African-black relationships in Atlanta, the immigrant group projects an image of superiority over native-born blacks; in this case, asserting their "ignorance."

However, most of the anti-Haitian sentiments I heard around the Quickie Mart were generated by whites. While three white male teenagers were waiting in line to pay for their drinks, a middle-aged Haitian man who had been attempting to use the copy machine looked up at me and shouted in a heavily accented voice that there was no paper in the machine. The white teens began loudly mocking him, yelling "Excuse me!" with feigned Haitian accents, then laughing as they exited the store. When I walked over to the copy machine, the Haitian man did not speak but pointed at the empty paper tray. I asked him if the machine needed paper, and he nodded in response. When I charged him for the copies several minutes later, he thanked me in an almost inaudible voice and quickly left. The tenor of this exchange was quite different from the conflict between the black couple and the Haitian man involving the car in the parking lot; in this instance, the Haitian man was shamed and silenced by the white teens. In addition, it is difficult to imagine the white teens making fun of a native-born black man. This particular group of teenagers regularly shopped (and shoplifted) at the Quickie Mart, and their primary targets for ridicule were women of any race and Haitians—never were black men ridiculed in any way.

In other cases, the heavily accented speech of Haitian customers resulted in misunderstandings with the cashiers at the Quickie Mart. These misunderstandings could quickly escalate into angry encounters, reflecting in some respects the misperceptions of prejudice reported in the last chapter. My favorite example involved a lengthy exchange between a Haitian woman who was buying two gallons of milk, Gus (the store manager), and a middle-aged white male customer. After I rang up her purchases, she exclaimed that she thought the price of the milk was $2.15. When I told her that the price had gone up, Gus piped up from the corner of the store that it was still the cheapest price in town and much cheaper than the supermarket down the street charged for the same product. The Haitian woman muttered something I was unable to understand, which prompted the other customer to tell her that she couldn't expect convenience stores to have the same pricing system. She responded that she wasn't complaining; she was getting the milk for someone else and didn't care how much it cost. Gus apparently misunderstood her, as he snapped at her again that there was nowhere that you could get milk any cheaper. The woman now became very angry and stated again that she wasn't complaining. However, both white men thought she was upset over the price of the milk. She stormed out of the Quickie Mart (never to return during my shifts), and the other customer told me: "It's a cultural thing; they're used to haggling over everything. But they need to learn that we don't do that here, that you pay the price that is marked." I stared blankly at the customer, while Gus continued to carry on about the low price of milk in his store. White men again projected a sense of superiority in this encounter; however, their comments reflected an anti-immigrant bias rather than an anti-black bias. The woman's behavior was discussed as a "cultural thing."

Part of the motivation behind whites' negative feelings toward Haitian immigrants is likely rooted in a sense of group threat. The white customer's comment about the way things are done here (as opposed to

Haiti) might have reflected a sense of invaded turf. The comments of two women who were regulars at the bar clearly reflected this sentiment. One of the women was discussing the fact that her leather jacket had been stolen at a Christmas party at the bar. Her companion commented that "people are coming into the neighborhood from all over. . . . You never know where they're from and you have to be careful." She made a motion as if she were glancing around and saying, "You know what I mean"; at the time, all of the other customers in the store were Haitians. On another occasion, a white woman who worked at a nearby nail salon commented on the silence in the store; we had been chatting for several minutes, during which no one else had entered. She said, "Everybody's leaving." After a short pause I nodded, and she said, "And the immigrants are moving in." She then covered her mouth with her hand, as if thinking she should not have said this. She quickly picked out a soda, paid her bill and left.

In other cases, the perceived threat to whites posed by Haitian immigrants is economic. One of the regular customers who frequented the bar across the lot, a white man named Jimmy, stopped in to buy some cigarettes shortly after a heavy snow began to fall one evening. He said that Gus paid him twenty bucks to shovel the sidewalks around the store. I told him I thought that was generous, as I was often required to shovel the walks for my hourly wage. Jimmy chuckled and began to reminisce about the racket that he used to have in the neighborhood; he would shovel the sidewalks for all of the businesses on the street for ten dollars each, undercutting his competition. He said, "But they're all new owners now, and I don't have many of the stores. A lot of the owners are Haitians and they'll shovel the walks themselves. They're too cheap." The net loss for Jimmy could easily have amounted to $100 per snowfall; given winter weather conditions in Boston, this was no trivial sum. In his perception, there was clear blame to be assigned for his loss of income: Haitians are "too cheap."

As was often the case, Gus stated the matter more bluntly than did anyone else. One afternoon shortly before the end of my tenure at the Quickie Mart, Gus had inquired about the "true" nature of my research, and I told him that I was researching racial attitudes. He became rather defensive, saying, "I'm not prejudiced. I just don't like foreigners when they think they are owed a job as soon as they set foot here and they can't speak English." Indeed, one of his favorite expressions to hurl at Haitian customers who caused him any "trouble" was, "What are you, just off the boat?" Gus had expressed prejudice toward blacks a number of times during the previous six months (as described in chapters 4 and 5); however, he was clearly aware of the social undesirability of these views. By differentiating black immigrants from native-born blacks, Gus was able to defend his behavior and attitudes toward blacks as a racial group by claiming his hostility was directed only at those who "can't speak English." Tonya, my white female coworker at the Quickie Mart, expressed the same sentiment after a hostile encounter with a male Haitian customer: "I'm not prejudiced or nuthin', but the guy has to talk so I can understand." Gus sardonically asked her if she were "making fun of my Haitian friends again."

A few of my observations from the Quickie Mart suggest that even other black immigrants looked down on those without a solid command of English. In the clearest example of this, Chad, a black man with a Jamaican-sounding accent, was waiting in line behind a black man who spoke limited English. This man was slowly selecting lottery tickets by pointing at them. He took quite a while to make up his mind about which scratch ticket to buy, and then it took additional time as I tried to figure out what he was pointing at. Milt, a middle-aged white man who occasionally worked as a bartender at the nearby pub, stood in line behind Chad. Chad rolled his eyes as the Haitian man finally completed his purchase. He then loudly told me that he was "growing a beard standing there." I told him I was sorry about the wait, but he told me not to apologize, that the "guy probably didn't speak English." I agreed, at which point Chad shook his head and made snide comments about Haitians to Milt. Milt burst into laughter, and the tension that had been building during the wait dissipated. Chad had waited patiently behind the Haitian man until Milt joined him in line. Chad apparently felt a need to demarcate himself from the inarticulate man in front of him; he had no sense of shared membership in the West Indian community (Zephir [1996] finds similar results in her study of Haitians). Chad's comments had their intended effect, as Milt recognized the boundary Chad had drawn between "Jamaican" and "Haitian" with his laughter.

OTHER FORMS OF DIFFERENTIATION AMONG BLACKS

Looming large in other processes of differentiation, especially those involving class and its cultural cues, were the issues of sex and violence. While whites in Atlanta often surprised me with their open expressions of contempt for poor blacks, this contempt paled in comparison to the derisions of poor blacks by the working-class black women at General Fuel.[6] "Ghetto" blacks were the most sharply drawn out-group: certain areas of town were avoided because they were too "ghetto," black customers who were rude or aggressive were derided as "ghetto," and certain places of employment were avoided because they employed "ghetto" blacks. While "ghetto" served as a loose substitute for "poor," it was not simply a marker for socioeconomic status or place of residence, but rather embodied a subjective set of behaviors and appearances from which many of the women who worked and shopped at General Fuel wished to distance themselves.

As was the case with whites in the Crescent, the greater the threat to one's own self-image, the more heated and vociferous the denunciations of those perceived as having lower status. This process was in full operation among the women at General Fuel. Many of the young and middle-aged black women I encountered hold the same negative feelings toward "ghetto" blacks that whites have toward blacks in general. Black men were commonly targeted for the most disdainful expressions, although women were put down as well.

Initially, such comments were made by only one of the cashiers, Madge, who is black and had grown up in a housing project in a predominantly white neighborhood in the Northeast. She had moved to Atlanta about five years earlier. At first I suspected her put-downs of black customers and other black cashiers had more to do with her attempt to separate herself from the others and affiliate with me, the white woman. While I still believe this is a partial explanation of her language, to my surprise, all of the other cashiers I worked with regularly as well as several of the regular (female) customers began to make such comments after they had grown more familiar with me. Molina, who herself was called "ghetto" by Madge and Telika,[7] was very circumspect with her comments about blacks throughout the first several weeks of my employment. By the end of my time at General Fuel, however, she routinely put down blacks she did not like with references to their "ghetto" behavior.

Terms such as "ghetto" and "nigga" are not necessarily derisive; they have worked their way into the everyday discourse of blacks in the Crescent (as well as those in Greenfield). The manner and context in which they are spoken is indicative of their meaning, which ranges from friendly affection to outrage. I specifically asked several of the women I worked with about this distinction, and they were explicit about the differences in usage.

Madge and Telika talked specifically about what being "ghetto" and "acting black" meant. "Ghetto," Telika said, "is a way of talking . . . like with lots of curse words." Madge said that there are times when she likes to "act black" or "be black." She said it involves "driving around, yelling at people I don't even know. Being ignorant, real ignorant."

In contrast to this negative definition, "acting black" was also commonly used as a synonym for "acting tough." Stephanie purchased a new pickup truck that she was extremely proud of; knowing a great deal about automobiles, she detailed the merits of her purchase. It was parked prominently in the front of the store, and she beamed with pride whenever anyone mentioned the truck. During one morning when business was uncharacteristically slow, Molina began to wonder "what if" somebody hit Stephanie's brand new truck. Telika and I cringed at the thought of it, while Molina gave us a demonstration. She said: "You ever see a white woman turn black? You'd see it. 'What, mothufucker? Whatchya doin', hittin' my truck?'" She made a fist, acting as if she were about to punch someone, screwing up her face in anger. We all laughed at her performance, although the demonstration evoked stereotypes of poor blacks as being violent and emotional and speaking nonstandard English.

Madge was also fond of giving dramatic performances when business was slow to earn Telika's and my laughter. One day she marched into the store posturing as if she was ready to fight. Jokingly she said, "Don't make me get black on you!" I do not believe that Molina or any of the other cashiers would officially endorse stereotypes like those posed by surveys, such as "Blacks tend to speak poor English" or "Blacks tend to be involved with drugs and gangs." Molina, for example, is an outspoken critic of antiblack prejudice and negative stereotypes of blacks. However, if the stereotype questions involved *poor* blacks as the target group, one might expect the endorsement of these stereotypes to be quite high among blacks in contrast to whites, who rarely make distinctions between poor and working-class blacks.

Madge asked Kim, a black cashier in her early twenties, to explain some of the slang terms that "black people" use, such as "buster," "boo," "youngin'," "shorty," and "gars." Madge kept reiterating how clueless she was about all of these words, about how she didn't know that "crib" meant "house" when she was young and told a man who was hitting on her that she "wouldn't fit in a crib." Kim and Telika both thought this was hilarious, but Sheree (who was twenty-four and was raising five children in a housing project across town) looked disgusted throughout our entire conversation. She sat frowning at us. Kim seemed to enjoy explaining all of the ghetto terminology, especially to me, and gave both Madge and me pop quizzes. My response to Kim's question about "ghetto" speech was met with raucous laughter from Madge and Kim; Sheree sat silently and shook her head.

I assumed that Sheree was upset because she saw my part in the "ghetto lessons" as offensive. As Madge and Kim were carrying on, I sat off to the side next to Sheree. I told her I didn't know about white people talking like this, that I thought such talk might be somewhat offensive. She started to nod quickly, and I asked her if that was what she thought. "Yeah, I think it's offensive. It's offensive for girls to talk like that no matter what. My sister is like that, like a tomboy, always getting into fights." I asked her if she thought it would be OK if a white guy talked like that; she thought for a moment, and then said, "Yeah. Yeah, it doesn't make any difference. I know white guys who talk like that." "Acting all tough?" I asked. "Yeah," she said, and nodded and started to smile.

Sometimes the expressions of negative black stereotypes did not appear to be attempts at humor or edification. For instance, a black female customer who regularly came into the store asked me if a black male customer in the store worked at General Fuel. I replied that he didn't but he looked like someone who did. She responded, "Well, they all look alike." Molina whirled around with an angry expression and responded, "You're dead wrong for that." The customer said, "Well, they *do* [look alike]." "You're dead wrong," said Molina again. This exchange illustrates a central tension in the attitudes of working-class black women toward poor blacks: a sense of solidarity juxtaposed with the impulse to differentiate. By applying a common stereotype of blacks, that they all look alike, without the spirit of humor that might characterize an acceptable exchange, the customer opted for the sense of superiority. Molina quickly attacked the customer for overstepping the line; her face hardened in anger, and she shook her head as she repeated the phrase she used when she was very upset with someone's behavior: "You're dead wrong." Rather than claim to have been making a joke, the customer instead defended her assertion. This was not necessarily an example of the internalization of a negative stereotype, as it can be interpreted as a put-down of black men who live in the area—the customer asserted that "they" look alike, not that "we" do. And while Molina could be quite harsh toward those in the area whose behavior she disapproved of, the use of such a put-down without provocation occasioned her angry disapproval.

As is common with many younger blacks, the men and women I worked with used "nigga" as a term of camaraderie quite often. More surprising to me was its use as a derogatory term (based on class appearance) or as a descriptor of skin color. I once asked Kim about her use of the term "nigga"—whether there were certain kinds of people that it applied to. She said "Yes! It's like, 'Hey Nigga! Whatcha wanta do 'bout it?'" (She pretended she was about to fight.) I asked if it was only used for men, or what. She said that it was used to refer to people who didn't dress very well or look very good, and that it could apply to women also. She paused a moment and said, "Although I usually refer to them as 'hos.'" I asked her if it was always an insult, because I sometimes heard guys calling each other "nigga" and it sounded like they were friends. She said, "Oh, yeah . . . it can be like, 'Hey nigga, wha's up?' It can be like what you call your friends. It depends on how you say it and who you say it to."

Molina would use the term only in reference to very dark-skinned black men she knew. For example, telling me about a guy who had been in the store whom she thought was good-looking, she said, "He's big, thick, black, *dark* black, and hairy. I like those niggas." While I never heard a woman referred to as "nigga," Molina and Telika once joked about being able to "act like a nigga," meaning that they were able to act like a man. They were referring to having sex for the physical pleasure of it rather than for any expectation of emotional involvement.

Since the term "nigga" causes considerable confusion for many whites who overhear blacks using it, it is worthwhile to provide some additional examples of the contexts in which it is used. One Saturday morning, a young white man who told us he was visiting from out of town asked Molina where the nearest "do it yourself" car wash was located. She replied that there were no such car washes located nearby. After he left, she told me in a hushed voice that she didn't want to send him to the car wash on Water Street (about a ten-minute drive away) because it was in a "bad" part of town and she didn't want him to get hurt.

She said she would want someone to do the same for her, to direct her away from a "bad white neighborhood." She said, "them big niggas would see him coming and say, 'We got one here—sucker.'" This exchange is notable for several reasons, including Molina's desire to be kept out of "bad white neighborhoods." She was defending her identification of certain black neighborhoods as dangerous for whites by asserting that certain white neighborhoods can be just as dangerous for blacks. Equally interesting is Molina's reference to the potentially violent blacks in the Water Street area as "big niggas"—violence, race, and masculinity are reflected in the use of the term.

WHAT DO WHITES MAKE OF THIS?

It is reasonable to surmise that many of the young and middle-aged black women I encountered view distancing themselves from the behavior of poor blacks, especially poor black men, as a strategy for avoiding white racism: if the burden of prejudice and negative stereotypes can be borne by *poor* blacks rather than all blacks, or by Africans or Haitians rather than native-born blacks, then working-class black women's own burden is lessened. However, this strategy meets with success in this regard only occasionally.[8] The reason rests partly with the subjective nature of such boundary drawing and partly with the very different standpoints from which working-class whites and blacks often evaluate others.

The only distinction whites made between groups of blacks was between "middle-class blacks" and "blacks." Middle-class blacks, with the exception of politicians, were admired by both whites and blacks in the neighborhood. The feelings toward middle-class blacks of the working-class blacks I spoke to and observed stood in marked contrast to their opinions about black immigrants or poor blacks. I never heard a negative comment about a middle-class black customer, not even about those whose behaviors I found rude. When blacks who had "made it" came up as a topic of conversation, they were always spoken of with admiration. A couple of cashiers spoke of having similar aspirations for their own families, and they wanted the freedom to move where they want and live the lifestyle they want without hearing negative comments from blacks who have been "left behind."

Kim, the black female cashier in the Crescent, prided herself on being tough; she gleefully described street fights she had won, and owned a small arsenal of handguns. Shortly before I left work at General Fuel, she participated in a boxing match sponsored by a local bar. She had always lived in poor or working-class areas of inner-city Atlanta or Washington, D.C. While one might expect a person with such a background to harbor some hostility toward the middle class, Kim expressed great admiration for blacks who had "made it." A newspaper article about Atlanta's black middle class prompted a conversation about class in the black community. Kim observed, "People who make money and move out are given a hard time, are called 'sell-outs'; people say 'Why you want to leave, forget where you came from?' But I think they should be able to live wherever they want, wherever they feel comfortable, as long as their personalities don't change."

Perhaps more surprising is the agreement of working-class whites on the subject. The black middle class (which is quite substantial in the Atlanta metropolitan area) was viewed with admiration. One white man who had made derogatory comments about poor blacks also said that blacks "who make it" could serve as role models for working-class white parents, with their emphasis on education and discipline. He cited the behavior of parents and their young children in the stands at his daughter's soccer games. He claimed that the black parents forced their children sitting in the stands to do their schoolwork, while the white parents were loud and raucous and let their children run around screaming. No such stories were recounted by the Boston-area residents, as Greenfield is not in close proximity to middle-class black neighborhoods and very few black middle-class customers entered the store (I judged by attire and speech in the cases where customers were not known to me).

In other cases, expressions of negativity by working-class blacks toward poor blacks were interpreted by whites as confirmation of their own negative racial views. This is especially true with regard to usage of the term "nigga," whether as a term of affiliation, description, or insult. Several male and female whites in the Crescent, but only one white male I spoke to in Greenfield, could not understand why it was socially unacceptable for them to refer to blacks as "niggers" when, they thought, blacks referred to themselves this way. Although the prohibition did not always prevent them from using the term, they felt it was unfair.

In most cases, whites observing black differentiation do not view terms such as "acting black," "African," and "ghetto" as anything other than synonyms for blacks. For example, Telika directed our attention one afternoon to an elderly black woman helping a child who looked to be about six or seven years old urinate in the bushes by the gas pumps. Since we had restrooms inside the store, the public urination was curious. Telika, Madge, Stephanie, and I were all staring at the scene when Telika asked, "Why is she making him pee out there? Why doesn't she bring him inside?" Madge replied, "Because she's black," meaning she was acting like a poor black. Stephanie's reply was, "That's not an excuse." Telika opined that the boy had probably done something wrong and the woman was trying to humiliate him by forcing him to pee in public. In this exchange, as in many others, "black" was used as a comment on the cultural characteristics of an individual rather than as a group or self-identifier; however, Stephanie used the term only as a group identifier.

The confusion is understandable given the complicated factors involved in defining appropriate and inappropriate cultural characteristics and the various terms assigned to people falling into different categories. For example, Sheree provides an interesting exception to the boundaries drawn between "ghetto" and working-class blacks along lines of socioeconomic status or residence. She began working at General Fuel due to changes in welfare laws that required her to work; she was in her mid-twenties, the single mother of five children, and had grown up in one of the toughest projects in the city, which had been razed a few years before she came to the store. She was unmistakably poor, but she was also very quiet and kind and projected an air of innocence. All of us were quite protective of her during her first few weeks on the job; even Madge refrained from her usual comments about "ghetto" blacks. Once, I found myself, inexcusably, hurling obscenities at a middle-aged male customer after he had treated Sheree so rudely she was almost reduced to tears. Telika tried to elicit some biographical information from Sheree one day when the three of us were on duty, including how she came to work at General Fuel. Sheree told us she had gotten a job at the retail chain Discount Clothiers, but had not taken it. Telika was outraged: "Why, girl? You know that's a better job than this one. That's a *corporation.*" Sheree was silent and stared at the floor. Telika's voice grew very quiet and serious, and she asked, "What happened, were you scared?" Sheree beat around the bush for a while, and it finally came out that she didn't have the right clothes to wear to work the first day and was unable to buy new ones. Her sense of shame and humiliation were tangible, and neither Telika nor I said much of anything for the forty-five minutes that remained on our shift.

I recount this negative case to emphasize that the put-downs occur and the boundaries are drawn not strictly along lines of class (poor versus working-class), but rather with regard to a complicated and subjective set of standards and cues. Behavior, dress, gender, personality, appearance, speech, and place of residence are some of the factors that trigger the use of terms such as "ghetto," "acting black," and "nigga." The distinctions have a normative rather than an objective quality to them.

RACE AND IMMIGRATION

While the conversations I participated in and overheard are certainly no definitive test of black boundary making, my observations do suggest that perceptions of group threat are a factor in many of the negative interactions between native-born and black immigrants. Rude exchanges in a convenience store carried a weight greater than mere social impropriety; instead, they became an assault on American culture and conventionally understood categories of racial identity, further evidence that one's group position was being eroded.

Survey results from the Multi-City Survey of Urban Inequality (Bobo et al. 1998) indicate that, while whites in Boston and Atlanta are roughly equivalent in their feelings of economic threat from immigrants, 52 percent of black respondents in Atlanta feel that present rates of immigration will result in fewer economic opportunities for blacks, while only 44 percent of blacks in Boston believe this. In terms of the threat posed by immigration for the political influence of each group, both whites and blacks in Atlanta believe that their groups will have less influence if present rates of immigration continue (54 percent of whites and 44 percent of blacks). In Boston 44 percent of whites believe that continued immigration will lessen white political influence, while only 26 percent of blacks believe this to be the case. While some of this discrepancy may reflect the relative lack of political power currently held by blacks in Boston, the gap in the amount of threat experienced by blacks in each city might also reflect the direct competition and hostile interactions with African immigrants that native-born blacks in Atlanta experience.

Nonetheless, old racial categories are undergoing a revolution of meaning in many cities across the United States, including Atlanta and Boston. "Blackness" is now understood by many to involve more than shared heritage—it encompasses, at the very least, a shared historical experience, shared cultural traditions, and a sense of group responsibility. African and Haitian immigrants are disrupting the meaning of blackness, much as Irish and Jewish immigrants once disrupted the meaning of whiteness (Jacobson 1998). The impact of this disruption on whites who live and work in the midst of blacks and black immigrants is varied; white Atlantans I observed treated African immigrants as no different from blacks, while white Bostonians clearly distinguished Haitians from blacks. Will new black-white alliances form in Boston at the expense of recent immigrants? Will African immigrants eventually have a harder time adjusting to a majority-black city like Atlanta than they would a city with a longer-standing multiethnic history? While it is certainly too early to provide definitive responses to these questions, the impact of African and Caribbean immigration is unlikely to be uniform across different receiving cities. Atlanta and Boston provide two models of the ways black immigrants are being incorporated into mixed-race, working-class neighborhoods, both of which suggest that the history of black-white relations in the United States will play a large role in shaping the adaptation of recent "black" immigrants to American society.

CHAPTER FIVE

Race, Crime, and Violence

Violence, threat, and suspicion surround the residential streets and public spaces of the Crescent and Greenfield. While crime is rarely far from the consciousness of the average American who watches the evening news, perceptions of risk and threat permeate daily life in many urban, working-class neighborhoods. Fear of crime is often overlaid with racial overtones, and it is easy to discern incidents of racial stereotyping among white residents in Boston and Atlanta. Some fear of crime is based in reality; according to crime statistics collected by federal and local agencies, the rate of violent crimes in Greenfield is almost twice the rate for the city of Boston as a whole. For the Crescent, the figures are even more striking: the rate of violent crime in parts of the Crescent is more than three times that for Fulton County, of which Atlanta is a large part. This is a substantial amount of crime, given Atlanta's distinction as the United States' most violent large city.[1]

Race and crime have long been bound together in the American public imagination, an association further solidified by rates of imprisonment that are far higher for young black men than for any other subgroup. Even across democratic countries, there is evidence that imprisonment rates are tied to racial and ethnic threat (Jacobs and Kleban 2003). In a study of arrest rates in South Carolina, a rise in black-on-white crime corresponded to an increase in black arrest rates, while no such increase was observed when black-on-black crime rates increased (Eitle, D'Alessio, and Stoltzenberg 2002). The media, especially local news broadcasts, have been linked to punitive attitudes among whites, although there is evidence that this effect is present only for whites living in racially homogenous areas (Gilliam, Valentino, and Beckmann 2002).

Convenience stores are notorious targets for armed robberies, and gas station attendants and sales counter clerks have among the highest rates of workplace homicide of any occupation (NIOSH 1995). On an average workday in 1995, two to three workers were shot on the job in the United States, at least one while tending a retail establishment (Bureau of Labor Statistics 1997). The reality behind these statistics was not lost on any of us working in the store, nor on many of the customers we interacted with. At General Fuel in Atlanta, customers confronted a three-sided enclosure of bulletproof glass that contained the cash registers and safe. Money, credit card slips, and packs of cigarettes were slid beneath narrow slits in the glass, one by each register. We cashiers referred to the enclosure as "the cage." The door of the cage locked automatically behind us as we left, and we were not to open the door with anyone nearby; at least one cashier had to be in the cage at all times. Video cameras were mounted from every conceivable angle, and the owner, Hank, reviewed the tapes at the beginning of each day.

The environment in the Quickie Mart in Boston was quite different, perhaps because a police substation nearby provided a greater sense of security for the manager. No bulletproof enclosures were to be found, and the single surveillance camera was wired to a VCR containing no tape. In addition, the cash register and store safe were located just inside the front door, providing a quick escape for anyone burglarizing the store. This relative lack of concern with security was crucial in facilitating several robberies, one armed, at the store in the several months I worked there. In addition, incidents of shoplifting and vandalism were so routine that the cashiers called the police almost daily. I myself called the police dozens of times during five months of employment.

While the choice of a convenience store as a research site may have made issues of safety and violence more salient than they would otherwise have been, the almost constant sense of threat felt by employees and some customers generated a set of visible, clearly articulated processes by which store visitors were evaluated for their intent to commit crimes. Race was one factor in these evaluations, although not simply in the sense of equating blacks, or even black men, with criminals. Instead, we invented our own brand of criminal profiling, consisting of a complex set of factors—age, gender, race, mannerisms, group size. For example, mixed-race groups of young men were scrutinized as potential criminals in the Crescent, while male teenagers of any race were closely watched in Greenfield. Even though the potential criminal was constructed differently in each store, in both places the process of associating certain types of people with the risks they posed involved a combination of on-the-job socialization and repeated personal experiences of witnessing crimes, both inside and outside the store.

We know a great deal about the negative effects of violent, crime-ridden neighborhoods on those who reside in them, and it is difficult to understate the power such an atmosphere has over the daily conduct of social life. Even though nearly all cashier-customer exchanges in both stores passed without incident, the tension generated by the need to constantly monitor the environment for potential threats produced an edgy suspicion. I found myself engaging in behaviors and making judgments that I would not have imagined before my tour of duty in the convenience stores. For example, I once sprinted out of the cage and out of the store at General Fuel to stop two men who were driving off without paying for their gas. After I hit the bumper of their moving car several times with my fist, they stopped the car and the driver came into the store to pay the bill. I was shocked by what I had done, which arose out of the frustration of watching repeated thefts and feeling taken advantage of.

In describing the powerful effects of crime and violence on life in the Crescent and Greenfield, I do not want to convey an impression of inner-city neighborhoods taken over by criminals. The vast majority of the people I encountered were not only law-abiding but also angry about the degree to which crime was tolerated in their neighborhoods. Stereotypes of "the city" as a war zone typically involve equations between the race and class of inhabitants and a propensity for violence, and a "ghetto" inhabited by poor blacks or Latinos is perceived as the ultimate embodiment of socially destructive behavior. While both Atlanta and Boston have areas locals refer to as "the ghetto," neither the Crescent nor Greenfield was considered a part of it. Both areas had significant white populations and were not especially poor, yet were just as affected by crime as many of the "ghettos" depicted in film and television as centers of violence.

THE DANGER OF CONVENIENCE STORE WORK

Working as a convenience store clerk poses its own set of hazards. The availability of ready cash in a location that is typically close to major roads has long made the convenience store a favorite target of criminals. Over time, cashiers develop a variety of defense mechanisms to manage an almost constant threat, including both a heightened awareness of the surroundings and a pose of toughness. This façade extends to store managers as well. Hank, the owner of General Fuel, would escort the assistant manager carrying money from the safe in the front of the store to the cash box in the back office with a loaded gun. On a day that the assistant manager was out of town, I carried the money to the office, with Hank holding his 9 mm Beretta in the air as we walked the fifty feet from the cage to the rear of the store. When I expressed surprise that he led me across the store with his gun drawn, he unloaded the weapon and let me hold it, explaining why this particular gun was the most appropriate for the job. He advised me that I should strongly consider carrying a gun myself, since I lived alone in a nearby neighborhood and went jogging in the afternoons by myself. He suggested a small-caliber handgun that would be light and easy to use. "You don't need to be Annie Oakley or anything," he said, but the small gun would enable me to "take out someone who was on the other side of the store."

The crimes that I witnessed while working as a convenience store clerk for just under a year ranged from the theft of a candy bar by an adolescent to a carjacking in the parking lot; the stolen vehicle was later used in a string of armed robberies committed across the state. I was not on duty when a gunfight occurred in the parking lot of General Fuel, and a murder at a nearby pay phone occurred just after I quit working at the store. I also ended my shift at Quickie Mart just over an hour before the cashier who relieved me had a gun stuck in his face until he emptied the cash register.

While I would leave all this behind in a matter of months, most of my coworkers had to devise strategies for surviving in this environment year after year. Some of these strategies involved rational calculations of threat and risk based on a variety of cues; other strategies involved humor, especially when the risk was great. The aforementioned gunfire in the parking lot of General Fuel took place during third shift (10 P.M.– 6 A.M.), and the black male cashier on duty that night, Antoine, excitedly described the scene to Molina as we arrived to start first shift. Enrico, a black man in his twenties who lived near the store and was an acquaintance of Antoine's, got into an argument with another young man not known to Antoine in the parking lot. The argument soon escalated, pitting Enrico against four cars filled with the other man and his friends. While clearly worried about Enrico's safety, Antoine laughed continually as he recounted Enrico's rash behavior: "Enrico was standing out in the middle of the lot, yellin' and shit, and there were four carloads of niggas in each corner! And Enrico didn't even have a gun! Goin' out there and startin' that shit." Molina seemed about to collapse she was laughing so hard, but she managed to yell, "Duck!" before she and Antoine laughed some more. While humor might not have been the strategy adopted had Enrico been injured by gunfire rather than merely scared away by it, in this case it provided a way for Antoine to process the occurrence in a way that minimized its impact, including any fear he may have felt.

Another oft employed coping mechanism is to cultivate an appearance of being even more threatening and potentially violent than any of those in one's environment. "Street culture," as this way of interacting with the world is sometimes called, has been most often recorded among nonwhite males in impoverished inner-city neighborhoods (e.g., E. Anderson 1999; Bourgois 1995). I witnessed quite a bit of this behavior among my female coworkers and among female customers—both white and black in both Atlanta and Boston. In some cases this involved "code-switching," similar to the shifting between "street" and "decent" behavior observed in Philadelphia (E. Anderson 1999). For example, Molina rarely put forward a tough pose, yet she could be just as hard as anyone at General Fuel. When she recounted her dispute with a grocery store clerk over the price of an item, she described her polite requests that the clerk check the price, including liberal uses of "please" and "ma'am." After the clerk responded in a surly manner (according to Molina), she leaned toward the clerk and said, "Don't make me get ghetto on your ass! Because I can do it!"

While Molina's dispute was fairly benign, other tales reported by my coworkers at General Fuel were more ominous. One of the youngest of the women who worked at the store, Kim, had moved from Washington, D.C., to Atlanta during the past year. Kim was black and openly gay and had a very friendly and open manner. She enjoyed regaling us with tales of her exploits in D.C., most of which occurred in a neighborhood that was almost entirely black and poor, in contrast to the Crescent, which had a sizable white population and a small minority of residents living below the poverty line. Kim said she used to love going into "the ghetto" in D.C. and getting her "folks" or "peoples" together and fighting. I said, "You weren't scared?" She replied, "Nah, not once they knew me there." She described the time she was walking in an especially tough D.C. neighborhood and a woman walking past her roughly bumped into her. Kim asked the woman, "What's up?" and the woman turned around and punched her in the face. She said she was caught off guard, and her lip was cut open. She and the woman then started "wreckin' it" (fighting). She went and got some of her "people," they came back to that part of town, and a large fight erupted between her folks and the woman's folks. The woman then showed her a 9 mm handgun and told her she would shoot her if she came back again. So Kim bought a gun and returned to the same street. When the woman pulled up her shirt to show Kim her gun, Kim did the same, and the woman said, "Oh, it's not like that," meaning she did not want to have a gun battle with Kim. While it is possible that Kim exaggerated some of the details of the story, it was unmistakably clear that she took great pride in ultimately prevailing in a battle of toughness.

Kim later asserted her toughness by participating in a women's boxing match held at a local club. While the usual weekend entertainment was ladies' strip dancing, the club occasionally hosted boxing matches instead. As Kim was bragging about how she would dominate her opponent in the ring, Tina, a black female cashier in her thirties, told Kim to be sure to have someone accompany her to pick up all the money that would be thrown into the ring. Clearly, the boxing matches were substitutes for strip-tease routines, yet Kim never expressed any desire to perform as an exotic dancer. The message of strength and toughness that Kim sought to convey with her public performance of violence was sexualized by the male club attendees in a way untypical for male displays of toughness; it is difficult to imagine an audience tossing dollar bills at male boxers in the ring.

Tina also warned Kim about the dangers of withdrawing from the match before a victor was declared. Tina had recently witnessed a near-riot at the club after a boxer's boyfriend stepped into the ring to stop the fight, as his girlfriend was being badly beaten. According to Tina, many members of the audience rushed into the ring and began beating the boyfriend; in the end, "they almost killed him." When I asked why so many of the men watching the boxing match reacted this way, both Kim and Tina said the audience was filled with dope dealers who wagered on the outcomes of the matches. Kim seemed excited by the added allure of the hair-trigger violence of the drug dealers.

Duane, my white middle-aged coworker at the Quickie Mart, endured almost weekly hardships due to the crime and violence in Greenfield.

He not only dealt with the same level of threat as a convenience store clerk that I did—he was the unlucky cashier who had the gun stuck in his face—but also was frequently involved in breaking up fights at the rough-and-tumble bar he tended as his second job. One Sunday evening he was groaning and limping across the store as I showed up to relieve him. When I asked, "What the hell happened to you?" he grunted, "Bar fight." He had leapt to the defense of a "young, small kid" who had said something offensive to one of the regulars seated at the bar.[2] Brad, the bar's resident tough guy, began pummeling the young man to the point that Duane feared for his safety. In attempting to pull the hulking Brad away from the victim, Duane threw his back out. He hadn't realized the extent of his injury until he woke up the following morning, and he narrowly beat the 7 A.M. deadline for opening the store (an alarm is triggered if the door is not unlocked by this time). I found such sacrifices for the sake of two low-wage jobs remarkable, but Duane seemed more concerned about "getting in trouble" for failing to open the doors in time than for injuring himself in the process of ending a serious physical assault.

After Duane's car had been stolen from outside his apartment for the third time in a year, he discovered that he was under investigation for insurance fraud. In addition, the thieves had removed the steering column, so he would be without a car for quite some time before it was repaired. Since all of this came on the heels of his back injury at the bar, I shook my head and asked, "How do you deal with all of this shit, man?" His response: "I drink, Monica, I drink. I'm just a drunken fool." While the strategy of humor is evident in this response, the humor is bittersweet. Duane really *did* have a drinking problem, and this was his dominant strategy for dealing with the numerous difficulties he encountered. He typically smelled of alcohol when arriving for work and would occasionally appear to be intoxicated. He narrowly avoided a DUI charge on his way to work one evening after being involved in a minor traffic accident; fortunately for Duane, the other driver was even more impaired than he was and drew the full attention of the police.

The most serious of the threats to the safety of any of the cashiers at either the Quickie Mart or General Fuel occurred less than a week before I finished my stint at the Quickie Mart. About an hour after I ended my day shift, Duane was robbed at gunpoint. I discovered this the next morning when I arrived at work to see Terry, one of the patrol officers who frequented the store, sipping coffee; he seemed excited or nervous about something, and he asked me if I had heard what had happened. He told me that Duane had been robbed at gunpoint, and I exclaimed, "Oh my God!" and pumped Terry for details. Since the Quickie Mart had no barrier between the cashier and customers, the robber could easily lean across the counter and stick the gun in Duane's face. In addition, the video surveillance camera that was intended to deter such incidents was attached to the tapeless VCR, Gus having apparently stopped bothering with the tapes some time before. Terry shook his head over the missing tape and said there was almost no chance that they would apprehend the thief.

When Duane arrived for work that evening, he described the matter-of-fact way in which the robbery had been committed, expressing surprise over the fact that a customer on the other side of the store had no idea what was happening until she arrived at the checkout counter and the robber had already fled. I asked Duane how he felt when he was being robbed. He said he wasn't worried or scared until after it had happened. The moment the police walked through the door, though, he said he began shaking uncontrollably as "the reality of what had happened" sank in. He took the rest of the evening off and proceeded to get extremely drunk with several of his friends at a local bar. When I asked him to describe the person who robbed him, he started out by telling me his height and then said he had "short dark hair, you know—an Afro. He's a black guy . . . ya know, he didn't look like anything different." He paused and jokingly said, "You know, they all look alike," and laughed. When he noticed I wasn't laughing, he quickly said, "I mean, he was wearing jeans and a plaid shirt and a jacket."

Duane seemed aware of the stereotype of the black criminal, and I felt he was trying to avoid a physical description of the man that included his race. He made a joke out of it, mimicking a commonly known stereotype that "all blacks look alike." When this strategy failed, he quickly moved on to an innocuous description of what the man was wearing.

I was warned about the level of crime by the managers of both stores when I was hired, although they emphasized the problem of theft over other, more dangerous crimes. When I interviewed with Gus for the cashier position in Greenfield, I tried to impress him with all of my previous "rewarding" experiences as a convenience store clerk: in addition to my experience at General Fuel in the Crescent, I had worked as a clerk in a store in South Carolina for two summers as a teenager. He chuckled in response, saying, "I guarantee you won't find this job rewarding." When I asked him why he thought this, he replied that it was "because of the kids" who would steal as much as they could as often as they could. If they got away with the theft, they would bring others to steal from the store, as well—"mothers, fathers, aunts, uncles, cousins, friends." Gus's prediction proved to be true, as teenage boys, both black and white, attempted to steal items from the store almost daily. In fact, controlling theft was the major and most difficult responsibility of the job. The cashier arriving for work would greet the cashier who was leaving with, "How bad were the kids today?" While such theft might seem a problem only for the store owner's profit margin, in fact it fueled a suspiciousness on our part that occasionally led to accusations of racism by young black customers, both male and female. Since these young black customers were used to operating in a world where black customers are held under greater suspicion than white customers (Lee 2000), the watchful eyes of white clerks were thought to reflect a racial bias. In some cases, race definitely played a role in clerks' evaluations of customers. For example, after I told Gus that a group of students from a local school had shoplifted a number of items en masse, he asked me if they were black. When I responded in the affirmative, he silently nodded and said nothing more about it. However, most of us cashiers were so accustomed to the thievery of youths of all races that we watched any male customer under the age of twenty for signs of criminal intent.

ANGER AND SUSPICION

In an area where crime, especially violent crime, is a constant possibility, suspiciousness is its natural concomitant. Race plays a major role in the evaluation of potential threat posed by either individuals or entire neighborhoods. However, in the Crescent and Greenfield it was not simply that all whites feared all blacks, nor that all blacks feared all working-class whites and their neighborhoods. Instead, each localized setting had a different set of informal rules that governed who could be implicitly trusted and who must be watched closely and carefully. These evaluations became especially important and refined in the convenience store setting, as crossing to the other side of the street to avoid a potentially threatening or unstable person was not an option.

During my first day on the job at General Fuel, I was admonished by Hank for not paying closer attention to a group of Latino construction workers who were selecting drinks from the large cooler in the back of the store. While I initially suspected that the workers' ethnic background motivated Hank's admonition, he followed his comment with a lecture on the danger of customers traveling in groups. At the time, I silently dismissed his advice, promising myself that I would not engage in profiling any customers. Wasn't fair treatment more important that a few stolen sodas? After several weeks, my attitude had completely transformed. Each minor shoplifting incident was experienced as both a personal betrayal and a reflection of my weakness and lack of street smarts. Incidents in which we apprehended shoplifters were relayed among the cashiers as heroic triumphs—we were cool if we caught the criminal in the act. Conversely, letting a customer "put one over on you" was a cause for shame. The unfortunate cashier on the night shift who accepted a counterfeit hundred-dollar bill was ridiculed and teased for her naïveté, while a male clerk at the Quickie Mart who routinely failed to prevent shoplifting on his shift was deemed "pathetic" and "lazy."

This concern with preventing theft in the store had little to do with securing the owners' profits; many of the same people who displayed vigilance while tending the register would themselves steal items from the store. Rather, the concern with loss prevention was a manifestation of our desire to be taken seriously rather than "dissed" [disrespected]. We could think of ourselves as tough, powerful, and in control of our environments if we could prevent the store—and by extension ourselves—from being taken advantage of.

Gus, manager of the Quickie Mart, would become especially enraged with the primarily white teenage boys who congregated in front of the store each day, periodically entering to occasionally buy but usually steal candy and sodas. He had prohibited two of the young men (one black and one white) from entering the store for any reason, and we were instructed to call the police if they set foot inside. The white teen would blatantly disregard the order, waltzing around the store, then parade up and down the sidewalk in front with his middle finger raised until the police arrived, at which point he would take off running. The charade would repeat itself several hours later. Dealing with him was frustrating in the extreme. One afternoon after several hours of putting up with the young man, Gus gleefully recounted the way that he had solved a similar problem several years earlier. According to Gus, he chased the boy on foot and cornered him behind a dumpster, where he administered a severe beating. A police officer interrupted the assault, at which point Gus explained the reason for the encounter. Recognizing the teenage boy as a habitual offender, the officer turned to Gus and said, "Good job," then walked away. Gus laughed heartily as he finished the story. One part of me experienced shock, and another part wished a similar solution could be applied to the current troublemaker. That I could wish for such a thing was itself a striking departure from the sentiments I held at the start of my work at the Quickie Mart, but weeks of being insulted and taunted with no recourse had left me in a vindictive state of mind.

I was able to see Gus in action one day when the teen who had paraded in front of the store with his middle finger raised decided to prance around inside the store again. When Gus yelled at the boy to leave the store, the boy offered his usual cheeky remarks and continued to walk around the store. Gus turned bright red, leaped from his chair, and lunged for the boy; at this point, the teenager decided to end the game and took off running. Gus followed him, yelling obscenities along the way, and returned a few minutes later out of breath but with a slight grin. He said he would beat the teen if he entered the store again and crowed that he'd "get away with it." Gus asked if the boy had been inside the store much on my shift when he wasn't around, and I responded that he had, numerous times. Gus became serious and asked me what I said to the boy; I responded, "I told him to get the fuck out of here." Gus's face lit up; he gave me the thumbs-up sign, said, "That was exactly right," and commended me for handling the kids much better than the white male night clerk, who was a quiet, submissive person. Taking the moral high road and treating the kids gently resulted in far greater problems than responding with toughness and rough language.

Customers, both white and black, had attitudes similar to Gus's regarding the teenage boys who congregated outside the store. One afternoon several of the boys began fighting with each other, and one of them was slammed by another into the wall by the cash register, knocking dozens of packages of batteries off their hooks. I walked outside the door and asked the teenagers to "take it somewhere else." When one of them responded by telling me, "Fuck off," I stared at him and called him a son of a bitch. To my horror, I turned around and almost bumped into one of the kindly old ladies who frequented the store. I turned red and stammered an apology for my language. Surprisingly, she jumped right in by telling me, "It's fine," that nothing else works with the kids. She began a long monologue about the irrationality of the young people who hung around outside the store; despite the presence of parks and youth organizations, the boys spent their days "bothering everyone." However, fear never entered into the concerns about the young people that customers expressed to me, and I felt only irritation toward them. While there was no group of black teenagers available for comparison, it is possible that the white race of most of the teens had something to do with maintaining a distinction between fear and annoyance.

Surprisingly, the most dangerous situation involving teenagers in the Quickie Mart parking lot was a near–race riot between a group of neighborhood white girls and a group of Puerto Rican girls from outside the neighborhood. The incident occurred late one Saturday night when Duane was working the cash register. Lisa, a tall, thin teenage girl with very light skin and hair, was a regular customer; she rarely spoke or looked up when buying soda or accompanying her white female friend who would buy them cigarettes. Apparently she had a disagreement with a Puerto Rican teenage girl in the parking lot that quickly escalated into a physical fight. After Duane broke up their scrap, each of the girls brought a number of friends to fight for her side. Chaos ensued, and the police had to be called to the area twice. The entire scene was an anomaly, as few Puerto Ricans shopped at the Quickie Mart or lived in the neighborhood and the neighborhood girls were rarely a problem.

Race played a major role in many people's evaluations of criminal threat in the Crescent and Greenfield. A few days after I started working at General Fuel, I met the store's maintenance man, Harvey. A short white man in his sixties with long, stringy white hair and a stooped posture, Harvey drove a beat-up sedan that he parked on the far side of the gas pumps, about three hundred feet from the store. One day, as I was sweeping the parking lot and emptying the outdoor garbage bins, I saw an emaciated elderly woman walking shakily alongside Harvey's car. The woman introduced herself as Harvey's wife after I nodded a greeting, and then she grabbed the sleeve of my uniform shirt (which rendered me instantly recognizable as an employee of General Fuel). She asked me if I would stay with her by the car, saying, "I don't know where [Harvey] is; he should be here." She looked around the parking lot nervously, and said there were a lot of people there she was afraid of; all of the people nearby were black men. I spent several awkward minutes standing with her by the car until Harvey approached us, telling me, "I got her. Thank you." He helped her into the car, and they soon left the store.

Harvey's wife clearly felt threatened and unsafe, even in broad daylight. Her fears were based on the cues she took from her immediate environment, which was populated by black men. None of the men I saw in the lot were engaged in anything other than the routine business of pumping gas and filling tires with air. Should one or more of the men have been behaving suspiciously, I would hardly have posed much of a deterrent. I interpreted her fear as reflecting racial bias, although I was unable to observe her in other settings, as Harvey never brought her with him to work after this incident.

More raw and overtly racist comments about blacks and their criminal tendencies were expressed by Steve, a skinny, middle-aged white man who was a friend of Doug, a white man in his fifties who was my main contact in the Crescent. When I told Doug that I was writing about the Crescent, he excitedly told me about all of the "characters" he knew whom he could introduce me to. One afternoon Doug stopped by my apartment with his mother and invited me to watch a "fight" between some white friends of his who lived nearby on a block that was primarily black. Doug told me several people would be there, including a "New York Jew, a prostitute, and a drug dealer." The three of us drove from my place, stopping to buy single beers to drink along the way. We arrived to see Steve loading a computer monitor into a small station wagon in the driveway of an extremely run-down duplex that he shared with his wife, Susan, a white woman who had grown up in New England and was a self-confessed alcoholic. While I am not certain whether Steve used or dealt drugs (he was not the drug dealer Doug referred to), I did see a crack pipe as I walked through the living room of the duplex. As we walked through the house, Steve said, almost by way of apology, that "this place is wall-to-wall niggers," motioning with his hands to encompass the block.

He later said that he was from a neighborhood in Atlanta that is now entirely black and poor but was predominantly white when he lived there in the 1950s. Doug followed up on Steve's description of the neighborhood by telling me that the projects which dominate that area were constructed to house veterans returning from World War II. Steve chimed in that this was why his father had moved them all there. He said he routinely works in the area now, primarily renovating apartments, and that he was not afraid of working in the projects (the residents were almost entirely black), because "you just have to know how to treat them. You go in there and act yourself. If it is your time to die, then it is your time to die."

While Steve clearly holds racist views, as evidenced by his unprompted use of a racial slur, he nonetheless succinctly sums up an attitude that is shared by many whites, especially white men: the black housing projects in Atlanta are places of extreme danger, where death lurks around every corner. This sentiment is all the more remarkable coming from a man who lived on a street with many poor blacks, whose own house was currently occupied by a known drug dealer who left crack paraphernalia lying around, and whose son was serving a prison sentence for armed robbery. Just a few moments after Steve's conversation about downtown Atlanta, an extremely large white man named Sam (a crack dealer, according to Doug) pulled a knife and held it to Doug's throat as we all were talking in the kitchen. Doug talked his way out of the situation, and everyone but I thought the interchange was funny. This irony would be repeated again and again as whites who themselves lived among crime and violence feared many black areas because of their potential for crime and violence. While I don't mean to suggest that poor black neighborhoods are free from crime—many have high crime rates—nonetheless, whites feared these areas to a much greater extent than primarily white high-crime areas, with "the projects" symbolizing danger and risk. This asymmetrical fear may be related in part to the urban whites' familiarity with the "code of the street" (E. Anderson 1999) that dominates their own neighborhoods. Conversely, their white skin might, in fact, put them at greater risk in majority-black neighborhoods, where they would typically be viewed as outsiders.

Most blacks I knew in the Crescent had a less alarmist view of the threat posed to them in poor black neighborhoods (all but one of the blacks I knew lived in primarily working-class areas, although most had grown up in poor neighborhoods). Yet they made a clear association between "the projects" and violence. For example, Madge, responding to one of Kim's stories about her love of guns, said she could never imagine firing a gun and that she didn't even like touching her roommate's gun. She told Kim, "I want ya'll to drop me in the ghetto and see if I can hang. Not the roughest ghetto, but just the ghetto." When I asked Madge where the ghetto was located in Atlanta, Sheree listed a string of housing projects (she herself lived in a housing project and worked at General Fuel as part of a workfare program). Kim interjected, "Shit, there's a ghetto right down the street." Everyone ignored Kim, and Sheree provided a ranking of the "best" and "worst" housing projects in Atlanta. Madge listened intently. All of the areas named by Kim and Sheree were entirely populated by blacks.

Among the whites I observed in Boston, the perceived safety of a neighborhood was highly correlated with race. Although criminal activity was a daily part of life in Greenfield, the perceived real danger always lurked outside the familiar local streets. Simply driving through certain predominantly black areas—much less living in them—seemed senseless risk taking to many Greenfield whites. For example, my white, middle-aged coworker Duane needed a ride to a local bus stop one evening and asked me which way I was headed to be certain that the bus stop was not too far out of my way. When I told him I was going to go up Lincoln Street to Peterson Avenue, which are central thoroughfares in predominantly poor black and Latino neighborhoods, Gus responded, "Lock your doors!" Duane suggested I take a different route, through primarily white and affluent neighborhoods. I tried this route one evening and found it twenty minutes slower than the Lincoln-Peterson route. I assume Duane suggested the route in order to maximize my perceived safety, as it was definitely no easier or quicker.

In Atlanta the perception of blacks and crime as inextricably linked is evident in the battles by white affluent communities to keep MARTA, Atlanta's public transportation system, from building routes into primarily white suburban neighborhoods. Fear of increased crime has been one of the primary concerns expressed by residents (Ross and Stein 1985).

However, Poister (1996) finds that the expansion of MARTA into suburban DeKalb County has caused no long-term increase in crime rates in the neighborhoods served by the stations. Similar findings have been reported in regard to the expansion of light-rail lines into affluent, suburban neighborhoods in Los Angeles (Liggett, Loukaitoui-Sideris, and Hiroyuki 2002). Little empirical evidence supports a correlation between the expansion of public transportation and an increase in suburban crime rates; these associations are a matter of perception rather than reality.

Whites in the Atlanta area have long joked that MARTA (Metropolitan Atlanta Rapid Transit Authority) stands for "Moving Africans Rapidly through Atlanta." The largely white suburban counties to the north of Atlanta, Cobb and Gwinnett, have their own transit authorities. Conversely, MARTA serves suburban DeKalb County to the east, which has a large black population. On the authority's web site (www.itsmarta.com) MARTA police have their own page complete with frequently asked questions, the first of which is "Is MARTA safe?"[3] In contrast, the web site for Metropolitan Boston Transit Authority (www.mbta.com) discusses safety primarily in terms of avoiding injury from the equipment itself or preparing for large-scale emergencies; the MBTA police force is not a prominent feature of the web site.

When I asked Sally, a middle-aged white woman who worked in the Crescent, about the reasons for the large increase in crime during the past decade, she showed a tight-lipped smile and said, "The MARTA line." I feigned ignorance and asked again, "So . . . crime has been increasing because . . . ?" She simply repeated, "The MARTA line." Sally never mentioned race directly throughout our conversation about the changes in the Crescent that she had witnessed during the past forty years since she visited her grandparents in the Hillcrest area of the Crescent as a child. However, she did say that the two developments that most dramatically transformed the neighborhood from the bucolic community she remembered to the crime-ridden area of the present were the expansion of industrial areas, which resulted in the destruction of a number of homes, and the construction of two MARTA stops.

While I did not spend much time riding MARTA myself, every time I was at one of the local stations I observed only blacks riding the rail system (the local bus routes were more racially mixed). I certainly interpreted Sally's remarks about MARTA as a code for race; unlike many of the men I spoke with, Sally seemed hesitant to mention race directly when discussing crime. In addition to MARTA, Sally also blamed the influx of drugs into the community as a primary contributor to crime so rampant that she would not let her grown children enter Hillcrest alone, much less consider living there.

Among whites in the Crescent, as well as throughout the rest of the Atlanta metropolitan area, there is a widespread awareness that the city's south side, including the southern suburbs, is less safe than other parts of the Atlanta area. A white repairman who visited my home one afternoon reflected this regional association, as he regretted not having moved "further south" than a nearby suburb when he left the Crescent. He had lived in Holton in the 1970s after returning from Vietnam, but had moved to another part of the Crescent because he "didn't like it" in Holton; he refused to elaborate as to why he didn't like it—he "just didn't." After he was forced to move from this home, he settled in a nearby suburb with a large black population. He said that he "hates it" there; when I asked him why, he paused and said that it was because "you can't keep nothing." He installed an alarm system, but "it doesn't stop 'em; it just slows 'em down."

The belief that predominantly black neighborhoods were unsafe for whites was shared by several of the black women I worked with at General Fuel. As related in chapter 4, Molina once falsely told a white customer from out of town that there were no self-serve car washes "around here" in order to avoid sending him to one a few blocks away in a predominantly black neighborhood. The car wash wasn't very far from the duplex I was renting, and I never felt uncomfortable walking by, and would have patronized it had I not received free car washes from General Fuel. In response to my surprised expression, Molina added that she would want someone to do the same thing for her, to steer her away from a "bad white neighborhood." Molina's comments reflect more than a simple equation of blackness with crime—she herself reacted angrily against whites who expressed this stereotype. Rather, she perceived real danger for a white man unfamiliar with the local streets and equated this danger with that posed for black women such as her in "bad" white neighborhoods. Unlike most whites in the Crescent or Greenfield, Molina made judgments about the susceptibility of particular individual whites to harm in some black neighborhoods, but she never issued warnings to me or any of the regular white customers about certain parts of town, and she expressed no concern about my living so close to the area she steered the white stranger from. At the same time, Molina had a subtle perception of the relationship between race and the "goodness" or "badness" of neighborhoods. For her, "bad" white neighborhoods would presumably be those she is unfamiliar with, as they did not include Holton, the predominantly white part of the Crescent where I lived. For Molina, who lived and worked in a mixed-race area, neighborhoods were judged as safe or unsafe based on an interaction between an individual's race and familiarity with the area's racial composition.

Not only were certain neighborhoods associated with heightened risk for whites, but certain times of the year were thought to be especially dangerous, as well. Stephanie and Hank told me about the worst times of the year for gasoline drive-offs: Thanksgiving, Christmas, New Year's Eve, . . . and Freaknik. Freaknik was an annual festival, ostensibly for black college students, held each April in Atlanta. During the late 1980s through the 1990s, Freaknik drew hundreds of thousands of revelers to Atlanta for what was essentially a massive street party, much like Mardi Gras in New Orleans. Hank asserted that Freaknik is the worst time for thefts at General Fuel; he has "every available cashier on duty because they [Freaknik attendees] would run off with the store if they could." Stephanie laughed and said that it gets really crazy and that I could see "naked black people" if I visited at that time of year. She described people urinating in public and women and men flashing each other. Unprompted, she added that "white girls are OK, but white men can't come into the city then." I looked quizzically at her and asked, "Why not?" She responded, "Because they'll get beat up." I asked, "But white girls are OK?" Stephanie replied, "Yeah, you know, they're girls, so people won't mess with 'em." She described the provocative styles of dress that the black female attendees of Freaknik wore, including very short shorts. Stephanie's assertion about the heightened risk for men goes against conventional wisdom about which gender need least worry about crime, especially with regard to interracial crime. Women are especially at risk according to critics of Freaknik, and arguments against allowing the event to be held in Atlanta center on the potential for violence against women. In years past, women have been groped and undressed by large groups of men. However, nearly all of this behavior has been directed at black women; this could explain, in part, Stephanie's lack of perceived risk for *white* women.

COPS AND PRISONS

Law enforcement officers were a routinely visible part of life in both Greenfield and the Crescent. A police station was not far from the Quickie Mart, and the store was a regular stop for two beat cops in the neighborhood. While General Fuel was not located so close to a police station, the store's easy access and free coffee attracted several of the local police regularly. Surprisingly, the first comment I heard describing harassment from the police was from a poor *white* man, Greg, who lived several blocks away from me in Holton. He appeared to be in his thirties, typically wearing dirty clothes and having an unkempt appearance; I would often see him walking with his young daughter to her school bus stop at the end of my block. He offered a warning about my out-of-state license plate by mentioning the trouble he had had with the local police as a result of his Alabama tags. Greg said he had been pulled over several times in the last several weeks, only to be let go after questioning with an admonition to properly register his car. He then noted that the police were really into harassing people in Holton. My neighbor Jerry seconded

Greg's assessment of the police; however, I never encountered any difficulties with the police during my six-month residence in Holton.

Several Boston police officers, all of them white men, were regular
visitors to the Quickie Mart. During a slow Sunday evening, I spent a
long time talking with one of the older officers, Terrence. He explained
to me the system by which officers are matched to specific patrol areas,
and I expressed surprise at his statement that most officers are allowed
to serve in the locations they request. I asked how the police force was
able to staff high crime areas given this policy, and Terry animatedly
responded, "They don't have a problem at all!" His first assignment was
in one of these neighborhoods, several miles away from Greenfield, and
his very first call was to a murder-suicide. He noted that he worked
there for over a decade and that officers select this assignment because
once you have handled this beat, you know "you can handle anything."
In closing, he mentioned in an almost offhand way that in this district,
"16 percent of the population is black, but 99 percent of the crime is
committed by blacks. Well, maybe 98 percent, but you get the idea." I
found this comment notable for several reasons. Despite no discussion
of race whatsoever in our long exchange about crime and the workings
of the Boston Police Department, the common association between
blacks and crime in Greenfield made its way into the conversation. Even
more surprising is Terry's estimate of the black population in his patrol
area and the amount of crime committed by blacks. He vastly underestimated the size of the black population and overestimated the amount
of crime blacks commit, although I suspect that he may have exaggerated these percentages intentionally. The exaggerations clearly con-
veyed the message that "blacks are responsible for crime." While the
racial attitudes of a single white beat cop are certainly not indicative of
a racist police force, I do believe that the ease with which Terry spoke
about blacks and crime reflects an assumption that such a view is
common sense. There was no awkwardness or hesitancy in Terry's
speech, and there was no need for him to bring up the matter of race at all.

Rather, he likely assumed that a fellow white person would react to such a comment as a normal part of the discourse about his job.

Reflecting national survey results, many of the blacks I encountered had considerable contempt and mistrust for law enforcement personnel. For example, one black female cashier who was hired shortly before I quit working at General Fuel responded to a news report on the radio with, "The police are like a gang, just like the Crips or the Bloods." However, I was unprepared for the degree to which many of my black female coworkers at General Fuel exhibited an extremely punitive stance on issues of crime and justice. The explanations of their "tough on crime" positions were rooted in a complex set of factors, including numerous experiences as crime victims, living in a hazardous environment, and anger and mistrust toward a number of the men in their lives. While none of the six women I got to know best on the job were hostile toward men in general, expressions of vindictiveness toward criminals were often supported with references to specific men they knew.

One afternoon I was leaving work early to present a paper at Emory University. This prompted questions from Rufina, a black woman in her twenties who worked the night shift, as to what my paper was about. I described the rather dry set of statistical analyses of class differences in political beliefs, none of which had anything to do with issues of crime or law enforcement. Rufina stared blankly at me as I finished describing my paper and asked, "Do you want to know what I think?" "Yeah, sure," I replied. In a heated tone of voice, Rufina said, "They should get rid of everyone in the prisons and give them the death penalty. Why should they get free food, they get to work out. Look at me—I'm late with a payment and they turn off my electricity." The other black female cashiers—there were six of us milling around since we were in the process of a shift change—murmured agreement with what Rufina had said. I was confused and surprised. Had Rufina somehow misunderstood what my paper was about? It was difficult to see how she could have, unless she associated "political beliefs" with beliefs about crime and punishment. I wondered if Rufina had perhaps gone on an anticriminal tirade because she thought that a white person would want to hear it. That also seemed unlikely to me, primarily because Rufina had never held back with her derogatory comments about "white music" or "white hair," both of which were certainly more racially loaded than beliefs about criminal justice. In addition, the spontaneous voices of assent in the background were hardly for my benefit, and it was not the first time I had heard a young black woman express punitive attitudes, although it perhaps was the most extreme.

Madge, Telika, and I were discussing different approaches to child rearing, with all of us bemoaning parents who spoiled their children rather than disciplining them. Madge provided two of her brothers as examples of the problems with an indulgent attitude toward children, noting that her youngest brother was always given everything he wanted and—consequently, according to Madge—ended up an imprisoned drug addict. Another brother of hers has "spent most of his life in prison." Telika responded, "Some people are like that, girl. Some people kind of like prison; it's a roof over their heads, something to eat, and a place to sleep." Madge concurred with Telika and mentioned that her youngest brother was able to send their mother more money as a prisoner than he was able to on the outside. Like Rufina, Madge and Telika viewed prison, for men at least, as a housing option—no bills to pay, no need to worry about having electricity or enough food. While this assessment certainly glosses over many of the stark realities of prison life, it is nonetheless a sad reflection of the degree of difficulty these women confront in their lives that prison can seem an easy way out.

Telika often provided a dissenting voice in discussions of crime and punishment. In one instance, she recalled her own ten-hour stay in jail in a city in the northeastern United States several years earlier. She had shared a cell with a woman who had just stabbed her boyfriend and the woman he was with. The woman was distraught, "cryin' and cryin'," and Telika said she "knew that I would hate being in prison after that." In contrast to the other cashiers, Telika identified imprisonment with her own experience as well as that of another woman who had struck out in a passionate rage against her boyfriend and his lover. Because Telika's empathy was reserved for the perpetrator rather than the victim of a crime, she served as a counterpoint to the punitive sentiments of her colleagues.

Telika and Molina both surprised me during my first couple of months at General Fuel with their ability to spot "ex-cons" who stopped into the store. In the vast majority of cases, the men were not known to either of the women; in all cases, the men were black. Whether their assessment of a customer's criminal history was correct or not, both women showed remarkable agreement in their evaluations. After the third such evaluation of a customer had been made, I asked Molina how she could tell a person was an former convict. She paused, as if taking a mental inventory of the cues that influenced her evaluation. She noted that the man had bulging muscles, that "his T-shirt was tucked in tight," and that he wore a belt. The bulging muscles were the ultimate clue for Molina, as these presumably resulted from many hours in a prison weight room. Without knowing with any degree of certainty whether any of our customers were former prisoners or not, I did begin to identify a certain type of man who had an intimidating presence but was fastidiously neat and polite. During my last month at General Fuel, Telika and I were working the cash registers one Saturday afternoon when a large, muscular, neatly dressed man politely paid for his gas. The second the exit door shut behind him, Telika and I said in unison, "Ex-con."

The high rates of crime in Greenfield and the Crescent, as well as the dangers of convenience store work, generate a series of assumptions of risk and strategies for dealing with violence. Some of these assumptions are strongly informed by racial stereotypes, while others are orthogonal to considerations of race. The assessments of criminal threat posed by individuals or environments are often subject to invidious racial distinctions. Whites may assume that certain predominantly black areas are extremely dangerous, even as their own predominantly white neighborhoods are rife with crime and violence. Regardless of their race, young men are often accurately perceived as the most likely to engage in criminal behavior.

As ethnographers of poor urban neighborhoods have found (e.g., E. Anderson 1999), those who must live with the constant threat of crime and violence develop strategies for managing personal risk. The most common of these strategies is to adopt a pose of toughness, whether through mannerisms, speech, or actions. This strategy was adopted by both blacks and whites and both men and women in Greenfield and the Crescent. Joking about the absurdities of senseless violence and posturing was another way of managing life in a high-crime area, as was the age-old "drowning of sorrows" in alcohol.

Relationships with and attitudes toward the criminal justice system were surprisingly complex, reflecting neither unremitting suspicion and hostility nor complete trust. While police in many areas have been guilty of abuses of their power, especially toward nonwhites, their ability to enforce any degree of order or justice in a community beset by crime engenders a degree of respect independent of their reputations. The same is true of the prison system: even though black men have been disproportionately affected by imprisonment, it was the black women that I worked with in Greenfield who were the biggest fans of long-term prison sentences. This attitude springs from a local context of frustration with the everyday level of threat posed by the environment; unlike some poor urban communities that have been all but abandoned by the police, the working-class areas of Greenfield and the Crescent both suffered from high crime rates and enjoyed a strong police presence. After having been robbed so many times that one feels "everything that isn't nailed down" will be stolen, residents seem reasonable in endorsing extremely punitive measures against criminals. While it might be more reasonable and effective to endorse the creation of jobs and economic investment in the communities, these solutions are more a part of academic discourse than of everyday discussions of crime and punishment in areas that see all too much of it.

CHAPTER SIX

Race, Gender, and Sexuality

Although I chose the convenience store as a research site because of its location as a public space where members of different class and racial backgrounds regularly interacted, I unwittingly selected sites that served as a locus for the selection and initiation of sexual relationships. In both Greenfield and the Crescent, flirtations and propositions between customers and cashiers were an almost daily occurrence. Conversations among the cashiers often focused on the attractiveness of potential or ideal sexual partners as well as the previous evening or weekend's escapades. Some of the cashiers and customers would not cross the color line; some would in theory; others had in practice. The pros and cons of getting involved with someone of a different race were much discussed, with the problems inherent in relationships with black men a common theme. While I initially tried to remain somewhat aloof from these conversations, telling myself I was there to study racial, not gender, attitudes, I grew to appreciate the remarkable window into beliefs about race that discussions about intimate relationships provide.

Nagel (2003) writes about the "ethnosexual boundaries" that pervade contemporary American society; not only are gender and race related forms of social oppression, but sexual beliefs and practices vividly mirror and help to generate attitudes about race. Certain groups that are both oppressed and feared, such as black men, are demonized as "hypersexed" creatures who prey on the vulnerable women of the dominant group. Such stereotypes are not merely the relics of Jim Crow–era propaganda, but continue to wield influence over behavior today; for example, Nagel notes that the gender imbalance among interracial marriages for different racial groups reflects cultural stereotypes about the sexual attractiveness of men and women of different racial backgrounds. Black men are much more likely to marry white women than are white men to marry black women, while white men are much more likely to marry Asian women than are Asian men to marry white women (Nagel 2003). Nagel notes that such patterns reflect an interaction between race and gender, as the gender balance among interracial marriages would otherwise be 50–50.

Ethnographers such as E. Anderson (1990, 1999) and Bourgois (1999) have described some of the gender dynamics in poor nonwhite inner-city areas, such as the need for male dominance over women in intimate relationships and the joy with which women greet the birth of a child, despite the economic hardship children impose. While I saw echoes of both of these dynamics in Greenfield and the Crescent, they were not at all typical. Perhaps because the neighborhoods I worked in were working-class rather than poor, they were characterized by different patterns of intimate interactions. However, I think most of the differences between what I observed and what other ethnographers have discussed were due to most of my conversations about sexuality and intimacy being with women. I heard detailed descriptions of ideal partners, sexual histories, and gender stereotypes from black women in the Crescent and white women in both the Crescent and Greenfield. Conversely, I typically heard only scripted comments from men about women, or observed them as they flirted with the women I worked with. Consequently, much of what I discuss will necessarily be slanted toward women's perspectives on sex, gender, and relationships, much as other ethnographic work by male researchers has necessarily been slanted toward a male perspective. At the same time, the portraits of sexual attitudes and intimate relationships I present reflect the comments and observations of a rather small, nonrandom group of women and should be interpreted not as *the* way that race and gender interact in working-class urban America but rather as reflections of some cultural images, stereotypes, and structural processes as they are experienced in individual daily lives.

Three major themes about gender and race emerged from my conversations and observations at General Fuel and the Quickie Mart. The first involves the ways race and skin tone influence perceptions of attractiveness. The white women I spoke with were uniformly opposed to having relationships with black men, while the black women I spoke with had a complex set of attitudes toward men that involved not only race but also skin tone. A second theme involves the wary, sometimes utilitarian attitudes many women had about men, which was often reflected in the way aggressive overtures by male customers were handled. More so than any other group, "black men" were an object of discussion and derision and were routinely stereotyped, especially by my black fellow cashiers at General Fuel. Finally, sexual orientation and displays of femininity among women at both General Fuel and the Quickie Mart were frequent topics of discussion, as the toughness many women felt a need to display on the job and in their neighborhoods was reconciled with dominant gender norms.

RACE AND SEXUAL ATTRACTION

Race repeatedly emerged during discussions of the sexual attractiveness of customers and ideal partners at General Fuel, due at least in part to the fact that these discussions often took place between white and black women, which highlighted the salience of race. I did occasionally overhear conversations between black cashiers in which race was mentioned, and I had conversations with white women in racially homogenous settings in which race would be discussed with regard to attractiveness; but these were exceptions. While I think that my presence as a white woman may have heightened the salience of race for the black cashiers I worked with, their comments about race and attractiveness were generally not flattering toward whites. Jan, a black woman in her late twenties who had grown up in the Crescent, was among the most vocal of the cashiers in assessing the attractiveness of customers after they had exited the store. One afternoon during her first week on the job, Jan was especially gracious toward a young white male customer whom I had never seen before. She gave him a big smile and greeted him, whereas she usually quickly rang up purchases without making eye contact or engaging in any social niceties. After the man left the store, Jan commented to me that "I don't often see white boys that look that good" and that it was enough "to make me convert." While I noticed nothing special about the young man's appearance, something about him prompted Jan to relax her usual race-based filter and evaluate a white man as physically attractive.

About a month later, after Jan had discussed her bisexuality with all of her coworkers, she, Telika, Stephanie, and I were chatting in the cashiers' box during a slow moment. Jan held forth on her assessment of the relative attractiveness of white men, black men, white women, and black women. In Jan's opinion, white men were vastly preferable to black men, while black women were more attractive than white women. When I asked her why she liked white men better than black men, she responded that white men "are more outgoing and creative," while black men "like to smoke blunts, drink, and do it all the time. They don't like to go out. Like I like to go to hockey games . . . and black men won't do that." While the stereotype of black men preferring to get high and have sex frequently was shared by other black women at General Fuel, I suspect that the unusual comments about black men not wanting to "go out" was said for the benefit of the two white cashiers, Stephanie and me. During my entire time living and working in the Crescent, I had never heard Jan or anyone else ever mention hockey, a sport that is played and watched primarily by whites. After Jan's comments, Stephanie interjected that she likes "white men better, too," then laughed. I followed up by asking Jan why she "liked black girls better."

Stephanie said, "Yeah, I was wondering that, too." At this point Jan, clearly feeling on the defensive, quickly backtracked, insisting that she liked white women as well. The conversation ended with Jan stating, "My last girlfriend was white."

Three weeks later, when Madge, Jan, and I were tending to the store one afternoon, Jan reiterated her preference for being with white men as opposed to black men by stating, "I would only marry a white guy," after commenting on the attractiveness of a young white male customer who had just left the store. As if the previous conversation had never happened, I again asked her why she felt this way. She again said that white men were "interesting," while black men did not like to do "interesting things." Madge mentioned that she too used to feel that way, saying, "I used to hate black people" (Madge herself is black). Again I asked, "Why?"—by this time with a look of surprise on my face, I suspect. She assured me that she doesn't feel that way anymore, since she'd met "all kinds" of different black people, and she concluded that "it's all background." Jan disagreed, reiterating her opinion about black men's refusals to engage in interesting activities: "No, black guys won't do interesting things . . . like mountain climbing." Jan selected another activity enjoyed primarily by whites and, again, never discussed by anyone I ever met in the Crescent. I told Jan that "middle-class black guys" will do those things, but she shook her head and insisted that I was wrong. When I told her that I knew black guys at Harvard who were into mountain climbing, she replied, "That's because they have money!" There are several interesting aspects to this exchange. The first is Jan's insistence on asserting that black guys don't like to do "interesting" things, activities that Jan herself had never participated in nor watched but associated with both whites and money. My attempt to make class distinctions among black men to explain a lack of affinity for mountain climbing appeared to make no difference to Jan, until it later became clear that "middle class" and "money" are not synonymous to Jan, while "Harvard," "white," and "money" were clearly associated with each other—and with activities that were "interesting."

Another time, Stephanie and I were discussing different breeds of dogs, and I said, "I love dogs." Overhearing our conversation, Madge interjected, "Then you should date a black guy." Stephanie and I ended our discussion, both of us in shock over Madge's comment. Madge quickly apologized and noted that she should not have said such a thing.

I noticed this distancing from negative comments on the part of other black cashiers, perhaps unsurprisingly. Often I would be engaged in casual conversation with cashiers during slow periods at the store when statements about preferences for black partners to white partners were made; when I responded with questions about the reasoning behind their preferences (I tried to follow any comment about race with further probes), it was as if the black women suddenly noticed that I was white and worried that I might have taken offense. For example, Madge made an offhand comment after a white customer left the store that she would "never date outside my race." After I asked her why she felt this way, she responded that she hadn't found the right person yet. I asked if she would date a white person "if they were right," and she responded in the affirmative. She quickly followed her comment by mentioning a previous girlfriend who was "an Indian." When I asked, "Asian or American?" she responded, "American," and went on to detail the "beautiful black hair" of her former partner.

Several weeks later, Madge expressed disapproval at Jan's stated quest to find a white person to date. She urged me not to take her the wrong way, as she liked an occasional "vanilla shake," but that it was wrong to select one's mate based on skin color. She finished by saying, "and you know I like my fudge." While skin color was clearly not irrelevant for Madge—she distinguished "vanilla" from "fudge"—she seemed genuinely to believe that racial background should not be a selection criterion for dating partners. Not so Kim, a black female cashier at General Fuel; she repeatedly stated her desire for white women to all who would listen. She said to Madge one afternoon, "I want a Caucasian woman . . . I mean *Caucasian!*" While she would occasionally comment favorably on white female customers, the only women I was introduced to that had gone on dates with

Kim were black. While Kim's comments about the desirability of white women may have been said at least in part for my benefit, in this case I was not a part of the conversation, but had been engaged in another activity at the edge of the cashier's area. Kim spoke about white women as she spoke about her potential boxing opponents—as people she would dominate and conquer. Whatever the reality of her actions, she voiced her desires openly and repeatedly to all of her coworkers.

I observed far fewer whites extolling the virtues of white men or women as potential partners than I did blacks expressing desires for racially exclusive dating, so I am unclear as to whether many whites in the Crescent or Greenfield would be similarly reluctant to claim preferences for same-race mates. The one example of a white woman blithely asserting her preference for dating exclusively white men is Stephanie, the white assistant manager of General Fuel; she never seemed to feel uncomfortable with her statements about her preferences, nor did she ever say anything positive about black men.

Gus, the white male manager at the Quickie Mart, would often make comments about the attractiveness of female customers, although usually not until they left the store. While Gus typically directed his comments toward white customers, he occasionally discussed the physical attractiveness of black women. In these cases, the women's race was inevitably at the forefront of his commentary. One day a black woman in her thirties made three separate trips to the store, although I had never seen her in the three months I had been working there. Gus joked with her that she was starting to become a "regular customer" and gave her a friendly smile—an unusual gesture on his part. After she left the store the third and final time, Gus turned to me and said, "I'd like to help interracial relations by plugging that hole." He laughed at my shocked expression and, without a trace of humor, meditated on the woman's beauty. He said she had shopped at the Quickie Mart the previous summer and caused quite a stir. According to Gus, the woman had been wearing a "tight white shirt without a bra" and "tight white shorts with no underwear." I raised my eyebrows, and Gus said he could tell that the woman wasn't wearing any underwear "because she was black and you could see her skin through the shorts."

Notable in this interchange between Gus and me was his need to introduce his opinion about the attractiveness of the customer with a crude joke about him doing his part to help relations between blacks and whites; the woman's racial background was highly salient and problematic for Gus. This is further evidenced in his description of the contrasts between the "tight white" clothing and the "black skin," skin that suggested to him a woman making a provocative presentation of self by not wearing undergarments. Gus made similar comments several weeks later when we were training a new white female cashier, Tonya. A middle-aged black woman who was a regular customer was shopping as Gus was eating his lunch, and he joked with her that he was eating salad because he was "saving himself for her." She responded somewhat sardonically that his comment was "very funny." After she exited the store, Gus turned to Tonya and me and snidely asked, "A little salt and pepper—what do you think?" Again, Gus's comments reflect the salience of race in his flirtatious interactions with black female customers.

A similar reluctance to consider interracial intimate relationships as a possibility despite a feeling of attraction was evident among some male customers at General Fuel. These white men would flirt with one or more of the black cashiers, then jokingly bemoan the fact that they were unable to date any of the women because of their different races. One white man in his twenties who was from the neighborhood stated this sentiment most succinctly, after having spent several minutes commenting on the attractiveness of Madge and Telika: "Why did I have to be born white with all you pretty girls around?" Neither Madge nor Telika responded to his question, although they did not appear to take offense. The belief that black-white racial differences posed an insuperable barrier to an intimate relationship seemed conventional wisdom to this white man. Indeed, very few interracial male-female pairs entered the store; such couples were much more frequently observed in the Quickie Mart in Boston, in every case a pairing of a black man with a white woman.

This conventional wisdom about whites exclusively dating whites was shared by my black female coworkers. One morning after a night spent on the town, Madge was regaling Jan, Kim, and me with tales from the women's club she had visited the previous evening. Turning to me, Madge said she meant to get me the number of a woman at the club, but she was "too drunk" to do so. In response, Jan asked, "Why, was she white?" Madge responded, "Yeah, real pretty, with long brown hair." Jan's question reflects the common assumption that whites date other whites; even though the club where Madge had been was primarily patronized by black women, Jan correctly assumed that the woman who prompted Madge to think of me must have been white. I had scrupulously avoided expressing any preferences for any type of man or woman, so the basis for this assumption was not rooted in any information about me preferring to date white women, but instead reflected tacit understandings about whites' racially homogenous partnering practices.

On another occasion Madge and Katoyah, a black female cashier in her twenties, were discussing music, and Katoyah expressed her admiration of Kurt Cobain, the late lead singer of the rock group Nirvana, who was white. She said, "If I were a white girl, I would date him." Madge responded, "Why can't you date him anyway?" Katoyah responded, "Oh yeah, I could date him, but I mean marriage and kids and stuff." Madge responded, "Oh, yeah." I stood silently off to the side as the interaction took place. Katoyah's fantasies about a dead white man illustrated the apparently widespread belief in the Crescent that "marriage and kids and stuff" should occur only between people of the same race; not even in the realm of pure fantasy about a dead rock star could marriage between a white man and a black woman take place. While Madge has rather catholic views on the matter compared to most of the cashiers and customers at General Fuel, she too conceded a line between dating and marriage that interracial pairs may not cross.

Most of the time, flirtations between female cashiers and male customers provided a way of alleviating on-the-job boredom. One white regular customer would always make a point of flirting with Telika, saying he was not content to leave the store until he could "see her pretty face." After he left, we would all joke about the man's bad teeth and Telika's power to attract unattractive men. Telika and Madge would often egg each other on during long Saturday shifts when the manager was not around. While their banter was usually directed at black men, occasionally other men fell under their gaze. A young man in a car with North Carolina tags who appeared to be Latino was paying for his gas one weekend when Madge told him that he was "sexy," primarily to show off to Telika and me. The man responded by wiggling his tongue at Madge and telling her to come to North Carolina, which led both Madge and Telika to begin screaming and laughing. After a brief discussion of how far North Carolina was from Georgia, Telika told Madge to get his phone number, but the man had just driven away. Telika said to Madge, "You just let my future husband get away." While their banter was not serious, at no moment did either Telika or Madge pause to consider the race of the man from North Carolina.

MALE-FEMALE INTERACTIONS

Flirtations between male customers and female cashiers were commonplace in General Fuel and the Quickie Mart. While these flirtations were frequently characterized by humor on both sides, occasionally a good-natured interaction could cross the line into something more menacing. For example, a large white man in his thirties with a blond crew cut who delivered merchandise to General Fuel several times a week carried on a flirtation with Telika. While this typically involved sweet-talking each other, smiling, and joking, the tenor changed one afternoon. After they had engaged in the usual good-natured teasing, the delivery man stopped in front of the register and simply stared into Telika's eyes, holding his stare without a trace of a smile on his face, refusing to break eye contact. After Telika started to back away nervously, he said, "I'm serious." It was then that I realized the teasing and joking must have been about some sexual topic (as it had been in the past).

Telika ignored him, and after he left the store, she shook herself and said, "Lord, I think he was serious . . . that was scary." In this instance, the delivery man's banter had changed in the space of a few seconds from friendly chatter between employees who crossed paths several times a day to an almost predatory stance toward Telika. Even observing the exchange from several feet away, I was taken aback by the delivery man's intense stare. From that day onward, Telika made sure to avoid the delivery man, and nothing more came of the incident.

It is difficult to convey the fear caused by what may appear to be simple miscommunication. A convenience store exposes the cashier to great risk of assault, as one is often working in an exposed setting by oneself and a wide array of men come into the store each day. As has been described with waitresses (Paules 1992), the job's public, service orientation can result in a greater sense of latitude on the part of customers. The dangers of the job were heightened at the Quickie Mart, where cashiers would often staff an entire shift alone and no protective barrier surrounded the cash register. Especially dangerous were activities such as emptying garbage cans that required a trip to a dark alley by oneself.

It is perhaps little wonder that Tonya, a white female cashier at the Quickie Mart, and I had many a conversation about men and safety. At times, these conversations had racial overtones, as when Tonya described two "black men" who had been harassing her at the store. Prefacing her comments with, "I ain't prejudiced or nothing, but . . ." she made a point of describing the "very dark skin" of one of the men who ogled her and repeatedly asked her for her phone number. When she finally gave him the number of a defunct pager in the hope that he'd leave her alone, he instead returned to the store and confronted her about the deception. She responded to his accusations with the defense that she was engaged and had two children (only the latter was true). But the man was undeterred, saying that he "still wanted to be friends." The same evening, she was deeply offended by a black man who had been lingering around the store, finally asking her what time she got off work. When she told him she got off at 6 P.M., he replied, "That's a half an hour after I get you off." Tonya said she ignored him, hoping he would leave. He finally did, but she clearly seemed shaken up by the incident.

On another occasion, Tonya and I were chatting as she finished her afternoon shift and I began the final evening shift, which included locking up the store at midnight when it closed. She said she would never consider taking my shift, as she was terrified of being raped while standing alone outside a dark and empty store. I told her I didn't blame her, as I had moments of being quite worried about the same issues myself. She surprised me by claiming that we could not even count on the police to protect us—before this I had never heard her utter any but supportive comments about law enforcement. When I asked her why, she described a white police officer who had been "hanging out" at the store for long periods during her shift, repeatedly asking her out on dates despite her refusals. He had been around earlier in the afternoon on this particular day, staying much longer than she would have liked. When she told him she was going to the bar across the street with her mother after work, he tried to talk her into going to a different bar, much farther away, with him. She refused by saying that she would not ditch her mother, and she went to the bar across the street as planned. I saw her at the bar on several occasions laughing and flirting with men there, but at the Quickie Mart she was always much more reserved and closed after this experience.

On the other hand, Stephanie, the white assistant manager at General Fuel, thoroughly enjoyed the attentions of various male customers. She was in a relationship with one of the white middle-aged men who worked near the store and went on dates with others. Molina and Madge joked that Stephanie could not be happy without a man, an observation that was borne out during my tenure at General Fuel. Stephanie would often amuse us with tales of her date the previous evening in a happy, animated manner. Conversely, all of the cashiers knew we had to be on the lookout for her temper, for if a man had not returned her call or had not called her after she gave him her number, she would be in foul humor the entire day. Without exception, the men that Stephanie dated were white. Nonetheless, she and Molina and Telika were united in their preference for "thugs," whom they described as men who would treat them "rough." The first time I overheard one of their conversations about the attractiveness of thugs, I asked in horror why they would *want* someone to hurt them. All three of them laughed at my naïveté, and Stephanie pulled up her pants leg to show me a two-inch scar she claimed her boyfriend had given her; as my jaw dropped open, neither Molina nor Telika seemed fazed. When I said, "You're kidding, right?" she shook her head and smiled, while Molina and Telika talked about how exciting a tough guy was. Stephanie admitted she eventually had to leave the boyfriend who gave her the scar because he had become "too rough," even though the sex was great. Both Molina and Telika nodded in assent, clearly bemused by my reaction. I initially assumed that the three of them were putting one over on me, but subsequent conversations and observations convinced me they were all quite serious about desiring "rough sex." While I am certain they are not alone in that respect, I remain shocked at the degree of openness all of my coworkers at General Fuel had toward discussing matters of sexual attraction.

At times, the misunderstandings and miscommunications related to intimate relationships took place among the cashiers themselves. One afternoon while I was standing quietly off to the side, Telika and Molina had an animated conversation about their preferences in male dating partners. Molina asserted that she would never date a man without money, that she needed to be certain that a man could support her before she became involved with him. She told Telika that she directly asks men about their financial situation before agreeing to have sex with them the first time. Surprised, Telika replied that she would never be able to ask men about their finances. After Molina held firm to her position, Telika said, "Girl, we'll start putting you out on the corner," in a reference to women who exchange sex for money. In sharp contrast to the good-natured tenor of their conversation up to this point, Molina responded with considerable anger to Telika's retort, as she was clearly insulted by Telika's equating her attitudes toward men with prostitution. The contrast between the two women is interesting: Molina was about fifteen years older than Telika and had consequently been through many more relationships with men, including two that produced children. For her, relationships with men could not be simply about feelings of attraction or lust; rather, she needed to assert control over the implications of her involvements by quizzing men about their financial security. For Telika, who was single and without children, dating men was much more about the feelings of the moment, with little thought given to any long-term consequences. While women with Molina's attitudes might be criticized as ruthlessly utilitarian, her reasons for adopting this approach to men were based on her understanding of responsible behavior, not on a desire for financially lucrative relationships.

While several of my black female coworkers resented men for leaving them saddled with children, it was white women whom I knew from the neighborhood who were the most forthcoming about sexism and discrimination they had faced as women. Sharon, a white woman who worked as a clerk in an Atlanta-area police station, described the intense hostility she endured from the police officers when she first began working in the 1970s. According to Sharon, the majority of the officers thought that a woman had no business in a police department, even as a clerk. Many of them refused her requests for paperwork because they refused to "take orders" from a woman. Ultimately the police chief was forced to intervene on her behalf, threatening the officers with suspension if they did not comply with her requests. She said that the situation for women gradually became more tolerable at the station as more women were hired.

SEXUAL ORIENTATION AND FEMININITY

As mentioned in the previous chapter, female cashiers often adopted a pose of toughness as a way of managing the high risk of crime in the convenience stores. This tough façade often needed to be reconciled with dominant gender norms that grant toughness to men and gentleness to women. There was little agreement about or open acknowledgement of these issues, although debates about the appropriate behavior for women did surface more than once at General Fuel. At times the discussion was couched in terms of sexuality, as two of my fellow cashiers at General Fuel were lesbians and one female cashier was bisexual. One of the lesbians, Kim, was very open about her sexuality and never exhibited any qualms about not fitting others' expectations of how women should dress, speak, or act. The other lesbian, Madge, and the bisexual woman, Jan, were more ambivalent about their presentations of self.

Madge informed me that she was gay after I had worked at the store for a couple of months and I had expressed interest in hearing more about several of the clubs she frequented. At that time, she told me that the only person she had discussed her sexuality with in the store was Telika, as she had not felt comfortable mentioning it to anyone else. This changed in the next several months, however, after Kim and Jan were hired. Just after Madge told me she was a lesbian, she admitted that she had never wanted to give birth to her child; she had planned to get an abortion, but her brother talked her out of it and raised the child virtually as his own. She abstracted from her feelings about her child to the general predicament that, according to her, many women find themselves in—pregnant with an unwanted child. She said that women get pregnant because "they want someone to love them" or because their husbands want them to have children; she implied that a genuine desire to give birth was lacking in most women. It is interesting that Madge's discussion of her unwanted pregnancy immediately followed her admission of her sexuality—almost as if the former provided an explanation or justification of the latter. Madge was not being self-critical, however, but was instead highlighting the social pressure on women to give birth and, by extension, be heterosexual.

In other cases, femininity is independent of sexual orientation. A vendor for one of the product lines sold at General Fuel would visit the store twice a week to restock the shelves her company managed. She was an extremely muscular, tall black woman in her late twenties or early thirties who participated in bodybuilding competitions. She always made friendly small talk with the manager and cashiers who were on duty, once sharing photographs of herself competing in a bodybuilding contest. All of this changed in the wake of a few minutes one morning about three weeks after I had started working at General Fuel. As the vendor entered the store, Telika called out, "How's it hanging?" The woman reacted angrily, stating, "It never was hanging!" While Telika was merely using the expression as slang for "How's it going?" the vendor interpreted the question as Telika poking fun at her masculine appearance. I suspect that the woman misinterpreted a rather common greeting as an insult related to the male anatomy because she was hypersensitive about her lack of femininity. Certainly, that was the way that Telika, Madge, and I interpreted the vendor's reaction. From that day on, we would greet each other with "How's it hanging?" then laugh and shake our heads.

Aside from specific individuals and their appearances, ideologies about conformity to gender norms were occasionally expressed at a more abstract level. For example, much to my surprise, in response to the Million Woman March my black female coworkers expressed uniform opposition. The Million *Man* March was thought to be necessary, but the Million Woman March, they thought, exacerbated problems between men and women in the black community. The radio show we listened to in the morning gave repeated updates from Atlanta women who had made the trip to Washington, D.C., for the march, so there was ample time to assert an opinion. Typically, Madge was the most outspoken critic, although the usually silent Sheree was also very critical. Madge thought the march was a bad idea, that women should "stop trying to take over everything." Both women thought that black women were too independent; Madge later said that black women try to do too much for themselves, saying "they don't let guys do things for them and then they're all heartbroken when he leaves them. I mean, I think women should do things for theyself, but not if it pushes everyone else away." Sheree verbalized her agreement.

Tonya's three months at the Quickie Mart in Greenfield that overlapped with mine witnessed her transformation from a vivacious, flirtatious woman who dressed somewhat provocatively to a defensive,

146 / *Race, Gender, and Sexuality*

anxious person who dressed in loose-fitting, heavy clothes to disguise her figure. In contrast to working at General Fuel, there were no uniforms to wear or dress codes to abide by at the Quickie Mart. Tonya and I compared notes on which clothes made the most unfeminine ensembles; I suggested the importance of heavy flannel shirts, while she emphasized loose-fitting jeans. I told her about the critical comments I had received from several of the regular male customers about my style of dress. She simply shook her head and reiterated the importance of dressing with baggy clothes.

One evening at the Quickie Mart an older white man from the neighborhood who visited the store daily to play the lottery asked, "What's the matter with you? When are you going to stop dressing like a truck driver?" I smiled and shrugged and began to wait on a middle-aged black man at the register. I noticed the black man staring at the lottery player, and as the door shut behind the exiting white man, the black man shook his head and laughed, saying, "I bet you hear a lot of that, don't you?" After my answer in the affirmative, he mentioned that he was very glad to be on vacation this week. He reported wearing a "nice dress suit" in his majority-black neighborhood, which bordered Greenfield, and noticing that people were really surprised to see him that way since his blue-collar job required him to wear work clothes. I responded, "You don't want to wear your nicest clothes to work since they'll just get messed up," and he nodded in agreement. He told me about the day he walked around his neighborhood "like this," imitating an exaggerated swagger, while also wearing old clothes and a baseball cap turned to the side. He said that a female customer he knew from his job shrank away from him in fear. He said to her, "Hey, it's me!" She then recognized him and said, "Oh, hello, I didn't know it was you." "It's funny the way people react," he continued, saying that he reassured the woman that he was not going to hurt her. He then said, "But you know, there's all kinds of stuff going on today, and people just don't know how to act . . . it's a shame."

I found it interesting that the white male customer's comment to me about my unfeminine outfit evoked both sympathy and empathy from the black male customer. Whereas I would not have considered his having frightened a woman with a streetlike swagger and outfit to be analogous to the exchange that I had had with the white lottery player, he clearly did. I inferred that the woman he interacted with was black, though he did not identify her race; the customers he would have come into contact with on his job would have been almost entirely black, like the residents of his neighborhood. Consequently, he did not racialize the incident but instead interpreted it as representing an unfortunate tendency of people to jump to conclusions about an individual based on his or her dress and style, with gender stereotypes playing a major role in the assumptions they make.

The relationship between gender, sexuality, and race is often subtle and complex—black men are alternately demonized and lusted after, while toughness and masculinity are both stigmatized and glorified, depending on the gendered and racialized situational context. Gender relations are also closely related to issues of crime and safety. The level of threat women perceive from men can lead to avoidance of or sensitivity toward race, much the way crime and race are shown to be related in the previous chapter. It is the subtlety of the relationships between race, crime, and gender that renders the detection of racial prejudice through direct questioning so difficult. None of the white women I knew claimed to harbor any prejudice against black men, nor would most of them even express an open preference for men of one racial background or another. Nonetheless, their evaluations of black men and white men often differed markedly, as did the evaluations by many of the black women I worked with. A set of assumptions and stereotypes were often far from conscious thought and were almost always removed from any understanding of what it means to be "racist" or "prejudiced." A kind of "free-floating prejudice" infiltrates many mundane interactions between blacks and whites, and attempts to lay it bare only result in defensiveness and a hardening of positions.

Conclusion

By the late twentieth century, the conflicts, animosity, and overt racism that had characterized relations between black and white Americans for much of the country's history were thought to be relics of an ugly past. Whites were responding to survey questions about the integration of schools and neighborhoods with unprecedented degrees of tolerance, and blacks were entering hitherto exclusively white workplaces and universities in ever increasing numbers. Yet there remains much uneasiness between blacks and whites in the United States; this uneasiness is partly reflected in continued racial segregation in neighborhoods and schools, substantially different political opinions and party affiliations, and periodic eruptions of violent interracial conflict, such as occurred in Los Angeles in 1995.

How are we to reconcile increasing tolerance and liberalism toward many matters of race with persistent segregation and violence? The usual methods of social scientific research have not found much evidence of overt racial animosity. Recent interview studies of blacks' and whites' racial attitudes reveal concerns with maintaining civility (Lee 2002) and moral boundaries (Lamont 1999). Trends in survey question responses show a stark movement away from endorsing traditional measures of prejudice (Schuman et al. 1997). Methods of direct inquiry are ill suited to revealing the often indirect ways by which race structures day-to-day life for both blacks and whites. However, participant observation methods enable the researcher to document the often subtle, subterranean ways in which antiblack prejudice can coexist with perfectly cordial surface-level interactions between blacks and whites.

After spending a year living and working in two predominantly white working-class urban neighborhoods that bordered predominantly black neighborhoods, one in the South (Atlanta) and one in the Northeast (Boston), I discovered that antiblack prejudice is alive and well. Race is rarely discussed by whites when blacks are present, and most whites are reluctant to make racially derogatory statements in front of strangers, regardless of their race. Furthermore, race is far from an obsession for most whites: instead, certain situational contexts and conversational topics, such as crime or schools, are likely to elicit racial stereotypes or negative comments. If I had not spent an extended period living and working as a member of the community, I would not have been aware of the extent of interracial antipathy, nor of its limits.

Interactions between blacks and whites provide a window into the complex, troubled history of race and inequality in the United States. Such interactions are often mundane on the surface but consist of continual attempts by all parties involved to decipher the intent behind words, actions, and gestures. When thousands of such interactions are observed in a natural setting over a period of many months, it is possible to detect patterns of behavior that reflect various contextual and situational factors.

For example, the meanings attached to white racial identity are not fixed but context-dependent; thus whites in two different neighborhoods that have nearly identical demographic profiles can have very different understandings of what it means to be "white." Whites in the "Holton" neighborhood of Atlanta have no sense of working-class or ethnic solidarity, but are instead aware of others' perceptions of them as individual failures for living in a city neighborhood on the less affluent, majority-black side of town. Whites in the "Greenfield" neighborhood of Boston feel relatively privileged, not only as whites but also as working-class ethnic whites with a strong positive identification with their neighborhood. In the Crescent, whiteness had an ambiguous status: in the aggregate, whiteness meant affluence, power, and privilege, but in the neighborhood, being white meant one had failed to live up to expectations. In Greenfield, being white was equated with power and privilege, if not necessarily affluence.

The different racial and ethnic histories of Atlanta and Boston also influence the ways whites evaluate black immigrants. African immigrants to Atlanta, a southern city with a history of Jim Crow segregation, are perceived by many local whites to be simply "black," despite the very clear distinctions their black neighbors and coworkers make between African immigrants and "blacks." On the other hand, whites in the port city of Boston, long a receiving point for immigrants from Europe and elsewhere, are clear to distinguish between "blacks," "Jamaicans," and "Haitians," with the latter group firmly anchoring the bottom of the status hierarchy.

In addition, certain topics such as sex, crime, neighborhoods, and schools were especially likely to elicit expressions of racial attitudes among the whites I observed in both Atlanta and Boston and among the blacks I had extended contact with in Atlanta. Black men, in particular, serve as a symbolic touchstone for racial stereotypes, fears, and misperceptions among both whites and black women. Especially with regard to crime, social class is virtually absent from considerations of risk of danger; instead, most of the discourse concerning violence, as well as other topics such as sexual attractiveness or neighborhood desirability, is racialized. "White" and "privilege" are so firmly linked, even in the minds of whites who are not themselves privileged or perceived as such, that race often serves as shorthand for class.

While some of these attitudes are detectable with traditional methods such as survey research or in-depth interviewing, others are so subtle and outside the immediate awareness of individuals as to be detectable only after long periods of repeated observation. By spending time working, living, and socializing with the people we study, by observing the "distribution of microsituations" (R. Collins 2000) among a subset of the population, we can gain a deeper, more sympathetic understanding of otherwise perplexing, even offensive beliefs. None of the "white racists" that I grew to know were unambiguously bad people; all of them could be thoughtful, generous, and considerate, and few of their insults or accusations were ever directed at children. Rather, they were reacting to the situations and circumstances in which they were embedded; race has been such a salient social factor for so long that it has become the filter through which rudeness, criminal intent, toughness, even lewdness are assessed and judged.

So how does race play out at the corner store? What is it about daily life in urban neighborhoods that shapes the way people think about race? In both the Crescent and Greenfield a free-floating prejudice surrounds interpersonal relationships. Interracial encounters are almost always polite, or at least civil, and race seems hardly to matter. Yet all this can change in an instant—a rude exchange at the supermarket or a misunderstood exclamation can set the stage for an exuberant display of antiblack (or anti-African or anti-Haitian or the like) sentiment. Fifty years ago a typical white woman ("Jane") interacting with a black woman ("Sue") and would see just a "black" or "colored" person. Since then, social interactions have radically changed. Now, Jane interacts with Sue as Sue—until Sue mentions her white boyfriend, or mistakenly insults Jane, or mentions the trouble her child has with the law; then Sue becomes a black person, and a whole set of group-based stereotypes can be activated. Conversely, Sue interacts with Jane as Jane, until Jane remarks about "those people" moving into the neighborhood, or shies away from Sue's hug or handshake, or mentions her black partner: then Jane becomes a white person, and a very different set of stereotypes are activated. This is not to say that antiblack and antiwhite sentiments are the same thing; they are not. However, the ways individuals become representatives for their racial groups is quite similar: certain racially charged comments or actions are necessary preconditions. While this applies to interactions in racially mixed communities, the effect of tokenism in racially homogenous situations would mean that the individual is almost always a representative of his or her race.

Long-term observations of day-to-day life and conversations, both intimate and public, reveal how whites and blacks often come to misperceive the intent of others' speech and actions. Blacks often fail to see the prejudice of whites, many of whom avoid the appearance of prejudice when blacks are present. At the same time, blacks sometimes interpret white actions as prejudiced when in fact these actions lack prejudicial intent. This discrepancy leads not only to misperceptions about the existence of racism and racial differences in both groups but also to potentially explosive situations. White hostility is most overt in the face of accusations of prejudice that are believed to be false, and blacks who discover the prejudices of whites who appeared to be free of discriminatory behavior experience a heightened suspicion of all whites. Repeated occurrences of misperceived interactions reinforce a gulf between the races that is difficult to breach.

The importance of white racial identity in mediating the expression of antiblack attitudes suggests that greater attention be paid to empirical studies of "whiteness." Survey research on *black* racial identity has generated a much larger body of research, especially with regard to theories of the black middle class (see Dawson 1994 and Hochschild 1995 for excellent examples). Theories of white racial attitudes can benefit from similar research. While whiteness often, if not always, is an objective advantage in American society, merely reiterating this fact will not help us understand why so many white Americans feel frustration and hostility that they often direct at black Americans. Analysis of the situations and contexts in which such hostility is expressed can help us to develop means of addressing racial conflict in urban America.

Furthermore, bringing participant observation research in multiracial communities to bear on studies of prejudice enables one to evaluate from a fresh perspective some of the major theoretical debates in the literature on racial attitudes. While much of the support for the "principled politics" of Sniderman and his colleagues (e.g., Sniderman and

Piazza 1993; Sniderman and Carmines 1997) is based on experiments with survey data, there has been little evaluation of their arguments based on other types of data. I found virtually no evidence of a politically principled stance on racial matters among the whites I observed over a year in Greenfield and the Crescent. Instead, whites in these areas were typically inconsistent in their outward expressions of prejudice, often making antiblack comments in certain situations but engaging in pleasant interracial interactions in others. Whites who discussed specific political issues typically framed them in racial terms rather than as appeals to abstract principles of fairness, morality, or individualism. A communitarian ethic (albeit bounded by race) rather than an individualist one motivated the beliefs and behaviors of working-class whites in both communities. It was the sense of being *white*—not of being American, or hardworking, or Republican—that drove the opinions of the working-class people I studied, perhaps because the whites I observed had numerous interracial interactions during the day and were thus more likely to be cognizant of their own racial identities.

The role of white racial identity as a partial determinant of whites' attitudes toward blacks fits best with the existing research on group position or group threat (Blumer 1958; Quillian 1996; M. Taylor 1998; Bobo 1988, 1999). The situational contexts and the tenor of antiblack attitudes expressed by whites in Greenfield reflect a clear sense of group threat, predominantly in the areas of jobs and housing. The role of group threat is perhaps more complex in the case of the Crescent, where many whites seem to feel ashamed of their racial identity. In this case, group threat conceived as *status* threat can explain the situational contexts and tone of the prejudice expressed by these whites. Blumer (1958) and M. Taylor (1998) specifically mention the theoretical importance of status threat in a model of group attitudes, although it has received little attention in the empirical literature, no doubt because it is a difficult concept to operationalize with survey data.

Additionally, a comparison of the results from Atlanta and Boston suggests that local context be considered when evaluating attitudes or behavior. The two neighborhoods in my study were selected so they were as similar as possible according to census data on income, education, occupation, and race, yet in many respects the residents' understandings of race were vastly different. These differences would be lost in a regression model that included only variables for income, education, occupation, and race of individuals or census tracts. I certainly do not suggest that we abandon statistical analyses of large-scale datasets in favor of case studies simply because complexity is necessarily sacrificed for generalizability as we move further away from the particular. However, I do think researchers (myself included) have come to reify variables such as race and education as representations of clearly delineated, consistently defined, self-aware social groups. Urban context is but one of many factors that can shift the impact of such variables on attitudes and behavior in radical yet potentially predictable ways. A broader consideration of contextual variables, such as the historical strength of labor unions or rates of European immigration, might lead to models that, by considering historical and cultural variables, better predict racial prejudice.

Experiences with race in working-class communities such as the Crescent and Greenfield take place against a backdrop of considerable stress and struggle. While life in these neighborhoods compares quite favorably to that in extremely poor areas, daily life is nonetheless *hard.* The financial difficulties and assaults to one's self-esteem posed by low-wage service work are difficult to overstate; Barbara Ehrenreich's *Nickel and Dimed* convincingly portrays the character of this work as filled with bleakness and uncertainty. Even for those with better-paid blue-collar jobs such as construction or factory work, the constant threat of crime, the lack of significant recreational space, and the general crush of traffic, pollution, noise, lousy schools, and limited opportunities take their toll. Perhaps even more damaging in the long run are the "hidden injuries of class" detailed by Richard Sennett and Jonathan Cobb over thirty years ago (Sennett and Cobb 1972). In many ways the most tragic aspect of inequality is the toll it takes on the self-respect of those outside the middle and upper classes. Behind the often brusque, occasionally arrogant exterior of those who labor for a living resides a well of self-doubt and fatalism. Men who on first encounter struck me as tough, conceited people would often put themselves down once I got to know them better, and many coworkers and neighbors who could exchange insults and profanities with the best of them demonstrated a startling lack of entitlement in matters of their own health or comfort. The many proud parents I observed speaking tenderly about their children's accomplishments and aspirations hoped also that their kids would avoid their own "dumb mistakes" and "screwups."

The depth of emotions, strength of stereotypes, and massive structural disadvantages that are evident in neighborhoods like the Crescent and Greenfield prevent easy solutions. A class- or neighborhood-based alliance across the color line is difficult to imagine in neighborhoods like Greenfield, although it is within the realm of possibility in areas like the Crescent. Perhaps paying closer attention to matters of white and working-class diversity could result in political or educational strategies that transcend current simplistic associations between whiteness and privilege while maintaining an appreciation for the larger context of antiblack discrimination in American society. Such strategies might ultimately result in everyday interracial interactions that are truly mundane and unworthy of study. If the status quo persists, however, interracial interactions will most likely continue to be fraught with misperceptions, accusations, and occasional overt conflicts.

CASHIERS, NEIGHBORS, AND REGULAR CUSTOMERS

THE CRESCENT

Name	Race/Gender	Age Range	Occupation
Blanche	WF	60s	Homemaker
Doug	WM	50s	Van driver
Jan	BF	20s	Cashier
Jerry	WM	40s	Truck driver
Katoyah	BF	20s	Cashier
Kim	BF	20s	Cashier
Madge	BF	30s	Cashier
Molina	BF	40s	Cashier
Sharon	WF	40s	Clerk
Sheree	BF	20s	Cashier
Stephanie	WF	30s	Cashier/Asst. mgr.
Telika	BF	20s	Cashier

GREENFIELD

Name	Race/Gender	Age Range	Occupation
Chad	BM	30s	Shipping clerk
Duane	WM	40s	Cashier
Gus	WM	50s	Store manager
Jimmy	WM	40s	Janitor
John	WM	70s	Retired carpenter
Milt	WM	60s	Bartender
Terry	WM	50s	Police officer
Tonya	WF	20s	Cashier

APPENDIX TWO

NOTES ON METHODOLOGY

While I tried to be as systematic as possible in designing this study, many uncontrollable factors in ethnographic research, from site selection to place of employment, render comparisons of interracial interactions in Atlanta with those in Boston suggestive rather than definitive. As with any study based on participant observation, my presence impacted the interactions around me and with me, as well as my own beliefs and interactional style. Finally, a number of other factors impinged on the quality of the observations recorded in my field notes on any given day, ranging from my energy level to the occurrences of major sporting events that influenced the size and composition of the clientele at the convenience stores in both locations.

The research in Atlanta was conducted between August 1997 and January 1998; the research in Boston was conducted between September 1998 and February 1999. I funded the research myself, based primarily on the wages I received for working as a convenience store clerk, which was perhaps not the best course of action; while it gave me a deeper appreciation for and identification with my coworkers, it also placed limitations on the extent of my involvement in the community, most notably by restricting the housing choices available to me. I ended up being priced out of the Boston neighborhood entirely; all of my coworkers lived with other family members who also had full-time jobs, which is how they were able to afford the local rents. Living outside Boston negatively affected the variety, if not the number, of the observations I recorded while doing research in Greenfield. On the other hand, I had more perspective on the relationship between Greenfield and the rest of Boston than was the case in Atlanta; living and working in the same neighborhood was somewhat isolating, and it may have reified "The Crescent" as more representative of "Atlanta" to me than it really is, especially given the area's unusual race and class composition.

In both locations, I have only limited insight as to the impact I had on the people around me or on the characteristics of the interactions I observed. Without question, my presence gradually became less noticeable and disruptive as time passed. This was reflected in the increased incidence of negative comments about whites in General Fuel and in the increased interactions with me (about any topic) in the Quickie Mart. In general, I was better able to "fit in" at the Atlanta site, as I grew up in South Carolina and had previously worked as a convenience store clerk there. I thus was able to speak and easily understand the local accent, and the fact that we were required to wear uniforms at General Fuel meant that I fit in with everyone else in terms of dress, as well. Despite having attended school in the Boston area for several years, I was much less familiar with local idioms and I did not have a regional accent, and there were no formal uniforms at the Quickie Mart to render me similar to my coworkers in dress. After a month or so, my coworkers and the regular customers seemed to enjoy having me around to chat with, although I did not get this impression at first; more than one of them assumed that since I was in school at Harvard, I would work a few days, then quit. When I began to catch shoplifters and worked a few night shifts by myself, I noticed that they were more open with me. I had the feeling that I needed to prove to them not so much that I was tough as that I was not afraid of mundane, thankless work.

I became much closer with a few of my coworkers at General Fuel—especially Molina, Madge, and Stephanie and one of the regular customers,

Doug—than with others in the Crescent. They shared intensely personal information about themselves, in some cases tragic stories of abuse and suffering (I did not record anything that I felt was a personal confidence not relevant to the purpose of the research); I heard some of this from John and Gus in Greenfield, as well, although it was less intense and less frequent. I was especially careful when leaving each site to have debriefings with these six people, but my departure from the field site was the end of anything that could reasonably be called a friendship. None of them found the nature of my research upsetting, or at least none expressed any negative feelings about it to me. Doug even insisted that I use his real name (I haven't). Yet there was definitely a feeling of loss for me, if not for them, when these relationships ended, and all of them did once the period of research was over. I don't want to suggest that the convenience stores played host to nothing but mutual admiration societies, but I do want to emphasize that the conversations I had with coworkers and customers in both stores involved much more than the conflicts and expressions of prejudice that I have focused on throughout the book.

Another factor that might have influenced the nature of the observations I recorded and analyzed was the degree to which my experience in the field changed my own opinions and style of interacting, so much so that I felt like a very different person by the time I completed my work at the Quickie Mart. I began my research at General Fuel believing that the criminal justice system was much too harsh on offenders, that people who were treated with respect would behave respectfully, and that the term "African American" was preferable to "black." None of these attitudes survived my period of time in the field.

For example, I gradually switched from using "African American" to using "black." I was corrected, more than once, by black cashiers at General Fuel when I said "African American"; the reasons they gave involved the desire to distance themselves from African immigrants. I realized there could have been another, unstated reason when I overheard a discussion between a white male customer and another white man at a drug store in the Crescent. The customer asked the other man, "Would he be an *African American* gentleman?" his voice dripping with sarcasm. The man laughed and said something along the lines of, "How did you guess?" Perhaps "African American" was turning into something of a socially acceptable racial slur. I have no further evidence for this, but hearing this conversation gave me pause, and I have tried to use the term "black" ever since.

Experiencing life in a virtually lawless community where many of the victims were black and most had moderate to low incomes, I was no longer able to maintain a simple critique of the criminal justice system as being too punitive; I now recognize my earlier beliefs as sustainable only when living at a distance from the constant threat of crime and its extremely disruptive impact on communities. I obviously am *not* asserting that the biases inherent in the current system are tenable, but I do recognize the arrogance of my earlier position. Similarly, I developed a new appreciation for the apparent rudeness of many cashiers, as their demeanor is a necessary psychic defense in the wake of the widespread ill treatment and disrespect hurled at them. I have no doubt that a similar shift in my demeanor occurred as my experience interacting with customers in urban convenience stores grew, which could be yet another factor explaining why it took me longer to have sustained interactions with customers at the Quickie Mart, as my time there began after months spent developing a defensive posture at General Fuel.

NOTES

PREFACE

1. Duneier's work (1999) as a sidewalk vendor has a similar approach, although his primary focus is on the impact of the enterprise itself.

2. My rather unambiguous "white" appearance—blue eyes, light hair, and so forth—gave me access to many of these conversations, which I would likely have been excluded from had my appearance been more racially ambiguous.

3. Such results may partly explain North-South differences in survey data in the endorsement of derogatory stereotypes of blacks.

INTRODUCTION

1. Kenneth R. Weiss, "Migration by Blacks from the South Turns Around," *New York Times*, 11 June 1989.

2. These efforts precluded my recording and transcribing conversations, which prevents me in many cases from providing direct quotations.

3. An exception to this trend is the more dramatic increase in support for having blacks over for dinner among southerners (Condran 1979).

CHAPTER ONE

1. In 2002, 6 percent of Georgia's workers were unionized, in comparison with 14 percent of Massachusetts's workers (Bureau of Labor Statistics).

2. Metropolitan statistical areas include a central city as well as outlying areas with "social and economic linkages" to the "urban core" (Office of Management and Budget 2000).

3. The index of dissimilarity ranges from 0 to 100 and measures the degree to which racial groups are unequally distributed across census tracts within a metropolitan area or city; the higher the number, the greater the segregation. The dissimilarity indices cited here are based on calculations by the Mumford Center for Comparative Urban and Regional Research at the State University of New York at Albany, available online at www.albany.edu/mumford/.

4. The Associated Press calculated a white-black dissimilarity index of 86 for the city of Atlanta in 2000.

5. I tried to compensate for this asymmetry in research design by spending all of my available time shopping and socializing in Greenfield. Ultimately, I spent approximately the same amount of waking time in each neighborhood, although the data from the Crescent is richer as a consequence of my having lived *and* worked in the same place. I do not think, however, that my conclusions would be any different had I lived in Greenfield, as none of my analyses of the Crescent were based primarily on observations made as a resident of the neighborhood; the vast majority of my field notes in both sites are from the convenience stores.

6. See chapter 5 for the negative consequences of this oversight.

7. I analyzed my field notes using the qualitative data analysis software package "Atlas.ti.," which has advanced coding and search functions that facilitate the development of theory grounded in the data.

8. The pseudonyms reflect the ethnicity of the actual names; for example, "Molina" is a nontraditional given name that would likely be identified as "black," while "Madge" (who is black) has a given name that is spelled conventionally and would not readily identify her race.

CHAPTER TWO

1. The perception of "Yankee" discrimination is intertwined with ethnicity, as it was chiefly Irish Americans who voiced this complaint, although one man of Portuguese ancestry did as well.

CHAPTER THREE

1. Such incidents were much more frequent in Boston than in Atlanta.

2. This is one of the arguments against the use of survey data to gauge attitudes.

CHAPTER FOUR

1. Other common U.S. destinations are New York, Washington, Chicago, Los Angeles, Minneapolis, and Houston (Paquette 2000).

2. Native-born black male limo drivers were also well liked and spent considerable time conversing with the staff at General Fuel, so the difference in the quality of interactions is not solely nor primarily due to gender differences.

3. The spanking may have been severe, as Tina later described pinching and twisting the arms of her neighbor's children when they misbehaved. Tina herself relayed being beaten so severely by her mother in a hospital emergency room that security guards were dispatched to the scene. Tina, aged twelve at the time, had just been informed that she was pregnant, and her mother reacted to the news with violence.

4. Strict child-rearing practices were observed with some frequency among Haitians in Greenfield. One of my coworkers witnessed a Haitian woman marching her three daughters into the store to apologize for shoplifting. After the apologies, she punched one of the girls in the chin and then told the clerk to call the police if the girls showed their faces in the store again.

5. I determined the ethnicity of the Haitian immigrants through their accents and, in some cases, dress; the Jamaican and Puerto Rican customers, through self-identification or identification by my white coworkers.

6. The cashiers' judgments about who was "poor" were highly subjective, but their criteria typically included some combination of unemployment, residence in public housing projects or dilapidated shacks, or receipt of welfare benefits (typically food stamps, as this was the most obvious public marker of welfare).

7. As Molina and I spent more time together, Madge referred to her when speaking to me as "your ghetto friend."

8. I don't mean to imply that this is a strategy in the sense of a carefully thought-out plan. Rather, these types of comments seemed marginally conscious attempts at differentiation and deflection, serving a purpose similar to that of the racist assertions of whites experiencing status threat (see chapter 2).

CHAPTER FIVE

1. In 2001, Atlanta's violent crime rate was 2,534 per 100,000 residents, compared to a national average of 504.4 (Morgan and Morgan 2002). Boston ranked thirty-seventh with a violent crime rate of 1,243.5 per 100,000.

2. He was a man in his twenties, not a child.

3. The response is neither a yes nor a no, but instead a paragraph about extensive police presence.

REFERENCES

Alba, Richard D., John R. Logan, and Paul Bellair. 1994. "Living with Crime: The Implications of Racial Ethnic Differences in Suburban Location." *Social Forces:* 395–434.

Allen, Theodore W. 1994. *The Invention of the White Race.* London: Verso.

Almaguer, Tomas, and Moon-Kie Jung. 1999. "The Enduring Ambiguities of Race in the United States." In *Sociology for the Twenty-first Century*, ed. Janet Abu-Lughod, 213–39. Chicago: University of Chicago Press.

Anderson, Benedict. 1991. *Imagined Communities: Reflections on the Origin and Spread of Nationalism.* London: Verso.

Anderson, Elijah. 1990. *Streetwise: Race, Class, and Change in an Urban Community.* Chicago: University of Chicago Press.

———, 1999. *Code of the Street: Decency, Violence, and the Moral Life of the Inner City.* New York: W. W. Norton.

Apraku, Kofi. 1996. *Outside Looking In: An African Perspective on American Pluralistic Society.* Westport, CT: Praeger.

Arthur, John A. 2000. *Invisible Sojourners: African Immigrant Diaspora in the United States.* Westport, CT: Praeger.

Ashabranner, Brent. 1999. *The New African Americans.* North Haven, CT: Linnet Press.

Atkinson, Paul, and Martin Hammersley. 1994. "Ethnography and Participant Observation." In *Handbook of Qualitative Research*, ed. Norman K. Denzin and Yvonna S. Lincoln, 248–61. Thousand Oaks, CA: Sage Publications.

Ball-Rokeach, Sandra J., and William E. Loges. 1994. "Choosing Equality: The Correspondence between Attitudes about Race and the Value of Equity." *Journal of Social Issues* 50(4): 9–18.

Barnes, R. H., Daniel de Coppet, and R. J. Parkin, eds. 1985. *Contexts and Levels: Anthropological Essays on Hierarchy.* Oxford: JASO.

Bayor, Ronald H. 2000. "Atlanta: The Historical Paradox." In Sjoquist 2000, 42–58.

Bennett, Gary G., Marcellus M. Merritt, Christopher L. Edwards, and John J. Sollers III. 2004. "Perceived Racism and Affective Responses to Ambiguous Interpersonal Interactions among African American Men." *American Behavioral Scientist* 47: 963–76.

Berger, Joseph, et al. 1977. *Status Characteristics and Social Interaction.* New York: Elsevier.

Bettie, Julie. 2003. *Women without Class: Girls, Race, and Identity.* Berkeley and Los Angeles: University of California Press.

Bixler, Mark. 1999. "Every Weekend across Metro Atlanta, African Immigrants Gather around Their Radios . . ." *Atlanta Journal and Constitution* (29 Nov. 1999).

Blank, Rebecca M. 2001. "An Overview of Trends in Social and Economic Well-Being, by Race." In *America Becoming: Racial Trends and Their Consequences, Volume One,* ed. Neil J. Smelser, William Julius Wilson, and Faith Mitchell, 21–39. Washington, DC: National Academy Press.

Blau, Peter M., Terry Blum, and Joseph E. Schwartz. 1982. "Heterogeneity and Intermarriage." *American Sociological Review* 47: 45–62.

Blee, Kathleen M. 2002. *Inside Organized Racism: Women in the Hate Movement.* Berkeley and Los Angeles: University of California Press.

Bluestone, Barry, and Mary Huff Stevenson. 2000. *The Boston Renaissance.* New York: Russell Sage Foundation.

Blumer, Herbert. 1958. "Race Prejudice as a Sense of Group Position." *Pacific Sociological Review* 23: 3–7.

———. 1969. *Symbolic Interactionism: Perspective and Method.* Englewood Cliffs, NJ: Prentice Hall.

Blumstein, Alfred. 2001. "Race and Criminal Justice." In *America Becoming: Racial Trends and Their Consequences, Volume Two,* ed. Neil J. Smelser, William Julius Wilson, and Faith Mitchell, 21–31. Washington, DC: National Academy Press.

Bobo, Lawrence. 1983. "Whites' Opposition to Busing: Symbolic Racism or Realistic Group Conflict?" *Journal of Personality and Social Psychology* 45(6): 1196–210.

———. 1988. "Attitudes toward the Black Political Movement: Trends, Meaning, and Effects on Racial Policy Preferences." *Social Psychology Quarterly* 51(4): 287–302.

———. 1999. "Prejudice as Group Position: Microfoundations of a Sociological Approach to Racism and Race Relations." *Journal of Social Issues* 55: 445–72.

———. 2001. "Racial Attitudes and Relations at the Close of the Century." In *America Becoming: Racial Trends and Their Consequences*, ed. Neil J. Smelser, William Julius Wilson, and Faith Mitchell, 262–99. Washington, DC: National Academy Press.

Bobo, Lawrence, and Vincent L. Hutchings. 1996. "Perceptions of Racial Group Competition: Extending Blumer's Theory of Group Position to a Multiracial Social Context." *American Sociological Review* 61: 951–72.

Bobo, Lawrence, and James R. Kluegel. 1993. "Opposition to Race Targeting: Self-Interest, Stratification Ideology, or Racial Attitudes?" *American Sociological Review* 58: 443–64.

———. 1997. "Status, Ideology, and Dimensions of Whites' Racial Beliefs and Attitudes: Progress and Stagnation." In *Racial Attitudes in the 1990s: Continuity and Change*, ed. Jack Martin and Steven Tuch, 93–120. Westport, CT: Praeger.

Bobo, Lawrence, James Johnson, Melvin Oliver, Reynolds Farley, Barry Bluestone, Irene Browne, Sheldon Danziger, et al. 1998. *Multi-City Survey of Urban Inequality, 1992–1994* [Atlanta, Boston, Detroit, and Los Angeles] [Household Survey Data] [Computer file]. 2nd ICPSR version. Atlanta: Mathematica; Boston: University of Massachusetts, Survey Research Laboratory; Ann Arbor: University of Michigan, Detroit Area Study and Institute for Social Research, Survey Research Center; Los Angeles: University of California, Survey Research Program [producers]; Inter-university Consortium for Political and Social Research [distributor].

Bobo, Lawrence D., and Michael P. Massagli. 2001. "Stereotyping and Urban Inequality." In *Urban Inequality: Evidence from Four Cities*, ed. Alice O'Connor, Chris Tilly, and Lawrence D. Bobo, 89–162. New York: Russell Sage Foundation.

Bobo, Lawrence, Melvin L. Oliver, James H. Johnson Jr., and Abel Valenzuela, Jr., eds. 2000. *Prismatic Metropolis: Inequality in Los Angeles*. New York: Russell Sage Foundation.

Bobo, Lawrence, Howard Schuman, and Charlotte Steeh. 1986. "Changing Racial Attitudes toward Residential Integration." In *Housing Desegregation and Federal Policy*, ed. John Goering, 152–69. Chapel Hill: University of North Carolina Press.

Bobo, Lawrence, and Camille Zubrinsky. 1995. "Prismatic Metropolis: Race and Residential Segregation in the City of Angels." Working Paper no. 78. Russell Sage Foundation, October.

Bonacich, Edna. 1972. "A Theory of Ethnic Antagonism: The Split Labor Market." *American Sociological Review* 37: 547–59.

Bonilla-Silva, Eduardo. 1997. "Rethinking Racism: Toward a Structural Interpretation." *American Sociological Review* 62: 465–80.

Bourgois, Philippe. 1995. *In Search of Respect: Selling Crack in El Barrio.* Cambridge: Cambridge University Press.

Brewer, John, and Albert Hunter. 1989. *Multimethod Research: A Synthesis of Styles.* Newbury Park, CA: Sage Publications.

The Brookings Institution Center on Urban and Metropolitan Policy. 2000. *Moving Beyond Sprawl: The Challenge for Metropolitan Atlanta.* Washington, DC: Brookings Institution.

Bryk, Anthony S., and Stephen W. Raudenbush. 1992. *Hierarchical Linear Models.* Newbury Park, CA: Sage Publications.

Burawoy, Michael. 1979. *Manufacturing Consent: Changes in the Labor Process under Monopoly Capitalism.* Chicago: University of Chicago Press.

Bureau of Labor Statistics. 1997. "Perils in the Workplace." *Compensation and Working Conditions.* Fall: 61–64.

Charles, Camille Zubrinsky. 2001. "Processes of Racial Residential Segregation." In *Urban Inequality: Evidence from Four Cities,* ed. Alice O'Connor, Chris Tilly, and Lawrence D. Bobo. New York: Russell Sage Foundation.

———. 2003. "The Dynamics of Racial Residential Segregation." *Annual Review of Sociology* 29: 167–207.

Clark, W. A. V. 1993. "Neighborhood Transitions in Multiethnic Racial Contexts." *Journal of Urban Affairs* 15: 161–72.

Clayton, Obie, Jr., et al. 2000. "Racial Attitudes and Perceptions in Atlanta." In Sjoquist 2000, 59–87.

Collins, Patricia Hill. 1991. *Black Feminist Thought.* New York: Routledge.

Collins, Randall. 2000. "Situational Stratification: A Micro-Macro Theory of Inequality." *Sociological Theory* 18: 17–43.

Collins, Sharon M. 1983. "The Making of the Black Middle Class." *Social Problems* 30: 369–82.

———. 1993. "Blacks on the Bubble." *Sociological Quarterly* 34: 429–47.

———. 1997. *Black Corporate Executives: The Making and Breaking of a Black Middle Class.* Philadelphia: Temple University Press.

Condran, John G. 1979. "Changes in White Attitudes towards Blacks: 1963–1977." *Public Opinion Quarterly* 43(4): 463–76.

Conley, Dalton. 1999. *Being Black, Living in the Red: Race, Wealth, and Social Policy in America*. Berkeley: University of California Press.

Cornfield, Daniel B., and Hyunhee Kim. 1994. "Socioeconomic Status and Unionization Attitudes in the United States." *Social Forces* 73(2): 521–32.

Cose, Ellis. 1993. *The Rage of a Privileged Class*. New York: HarperCollins.

Cotter, David A., Joan M. Hermsen, and Reeve Vanneman. 2003. "The Effects of Occupational Gender Segregation across Race." *Sociological Quarterly* 44(1):17–36.

Cotton, Jeremiah. 1990. "The Gap at the Top: Relative Occupational Earnings Disadvantages of the Black Middle Class." *Review of Black Political Economy* 18: 21–38.

Creswell, John W. 1994. *Research Design: Qualitative and Quantitative Approaches*. Thousand Oaks, CA: Sage Publications.

Daniels, Jessie. 1997. *White Lies: Race, Class, Gender, and Sexuality in White Supremacist Discourse*. New York: Routledge.

Davis, James A. 1982. "Achievement Variables and Class Cultures: Family, Schooling, Job, and Forty-Nine Dependent Variables in the Cumulative GSS." *American Sociological Review* 47: 569–86.

Dawson, Michael. 1994. *Behind the Mule: Race and Class in African-American Politics*. Princeton, NJ: Princeton University Press.

DeAndrade, Lelia Lomba. 2000. "Negotiating from the Inside: Constructing Racial and Ethnic Identity in Qualitative Research." *Journal of Contemporary Ethnography* 29: 268–90.

Delaney, D. 2002. "The Space That Race Makes." *Professional Geographer* 54: 6–14.

Dillingham, Gerald L. 1981. "The Emerging Black Middle Class: Class Conscious or Race Conscious?" *Ethnic and Racial Studies* 4: 432–49.

Djamba, Y. K. 1999. "African Immigrants in the United States: A Socio-demographic Profile in Comparison to Native Blacks." *Journal of Asian and African Studies* 34: 210–15.

Dodoo, F. Nii-Amoo. 1997. "Assimilation Differences among Africans in America." *Social Forces* 76: 527–46.

Duckitt, John. 1992. *The Social Psychology of Prejudice*. New York: Praeger.

Duneier, Mitchell. 1999. *Sidewalk*. New York: Farrar, Straus and Giroux.

Durant, Thomas J., Jr., and Joyce S. Louden. 1986. "The Black Middle Class in America: Historical and Contemporary Perspectives." *Phylon* 47: 253–63.

Durr, Kenneth D. 2003. *Behind the Backlash: White Working-Class Politics in Baltimore, 1940–1980*. Chapel Hill: University of North Carolina Press.

Dymski, Gary A. 1992. "Towards a New Model of Exploitation: The Case of Racial Domination." *International Journal of Social Economics* 19: 292.

Edgar, Walter. 1999. "Beyond the Tumult and the Shouting: Black and White in South Carolina in the 1990's." In *The Southern State of Mind*, ed. Jan Nordby Gretlund. Columbia: University of South Carolina Press.

Ehrenreich, Barbara. 2001. *Nickel and Dimed: On (Not) Getting By in Boom-Time America*. New York: Henry Holt.

Eitle, David, Stewart J. D'Alessio, and Lisa Stoltzenberg. 2002. "Racial Threat and Social Control: A Test of the Political, Economic and Threat of Black Crime Hypotheses. *Social Forces* 81(2): 557–76.

Eitle, David, and Tamela McNulty Eitle. 2003. "Segregation and School Violence." *Social Forces* 84(2): 589–615.

Ellen, Ingrid Gould, and Margery Ellen Turner. 1997. "Does Neighborhood Matter? Assessing Recent Evidence." *Housing Policy Debate* 8(4): 833–66.

Ellison, Christopher G., and Marc A. Musick. 1993. "Southern Intolerance: A Fundamentalist Effect?" *Social Forces* 72(2): 379–98.

Ellison, Christopher G., and Daniel A. Powers. 1994. "The Contact Hypothesis and Racial Attitudes among Black Americans." *Social Science Quarterly* 75(2): 385–400.

Emig, Arthur G., et al. 1996. "Black-White Differences in Political Efficacy, Trust, and Sociopolitical Participation: A Critique of the Empowerment Hypothesis." *Urban Affairs Review* 32(2): 264–76.

Entwisle, Doris, and Karl Alexander. 1992. "Summer Setback: Race, Poverty, School Composition, and Mathematics Achievement in the First Two Years of School." *American Sociological Review* 57: 72–84.

Erbe, Brigitte M. 1975. "Race and Socioeconomic Segregation." *American Sociological Review* 40: 801–12.

Farley, Reynolds. 1982. *Blacks and Whites*. Cambridge, MA: Harvard University Press.

Farley, Reynolds, Suzanne Bianchi, and Diane Colasanto. 1979. "Barriers to the Racial Integration of Neighborhoods: The Detroit Case." *Annals of the American Academy of Political and Social Sciences* 441: 97–113.

Farley, Reynolds, Sheldon D. Danziger, and Harry J. Holzer. 2000. *Detroit Divided: Racial and Spatial Inequalities in Employment and Housing*. New York: Russell Sage Foundation.

Farley, Reynolds, Elaine L. Fielding, and Maria Krysan. 1997. "The Residential Preferences of Blacks and Whites: A Four Metropolis Analysis." *Housing Policy Debate* 8(4): 763–800.

Farley, Reynolds, and William H. Frey. 1994. "Changes in the Segregation of Whites from Blacks during the 1980's." *American Sociological Review* 59: 23–45.

Farley, Reynolds, Howard Schuman, Suzanne Bianchi, Diane Colasanto, and Shirley Hatchett. 1978. "'Chocolate Cities, Vanilla Suburbs': Will the Trend toward Racially Separate Communities Continue?" *Social Science Research* 7: 335.

Feagin, Joe R. 1991. "The Continuing Significance of Race: Antiblack Discrimination in Public Places." *American Sociological Review* 56: 101–16.

———. 2000. *Racist America: Roots, Current Realities and Future Reparations.* New York: Routledge.

Feagin, Joe R., and Melvin T. Sikes. 1994. *Living with Racism: The Black Middle Class Experience.* Boston: Beacon Press.

Fine, Gary Alan, and Patricia A. Turner. 2001. *Whispers on the Color Line: Rumor and Race in America.* Berkeley and Los Angeles: University of California Press.

Finlay, Nikki McIntyre. 2000. "Finding Work in Atlanta: Is There an Optimal Strategy for Disadvantaged Job Seekers?" In Sjoquist 2000, 217–43.

Fordham, Signithia. 1988. "Racelessness as a Factor in Black Students' School Success: Pragmatic Strategy or Pyrrhic Victory?" *Harvard Educational Review* 58: 54–84.

Formisano, Ronald P. 1991. *Boston Against Busing: Race, Class and Ethnicity in the 1960s and 1970s.* Chapel Hill: University of North Carolina Press.

Fossett, Mark A., and K. Jill Kiecolt. 1989. "The Relative Size of Minority Populations and White Racial Attitudes." *Social Science Quarterly* 70: 820–35.

Frankenberg, Ruth, ed. 1997. *Displacing Whiteness: Essays in Social and Cultural Criticism.* Durham, NC: Duke University Press.

Franklin, Raymond S. 1991. *Shadows of Race and Class.* Minneapolis: University of Minnesota Press.

Frazier, E. Franklin. 1957. *Black Bourgeoisie.* Glencoe, IL: Free Press.

Geschwender, James A. 1988. "The Portuguese and Haoles of Hawaii: Implications for the Origin of Ethnicity." *American Sociological Review* 53: 515–27.

Gilens, Martin. 1995. "Racial Attitudes and Opposition to Welfare." *Journal of Politics* 57: 994–1014.

———. 1999. *Why Americans Hate Welfare.* Chicago: University of Chicago Press.

Giles, Michael W. 1977. "Percent Black and Racial Hostility: An Old Assumption Reexamined." *Social Science Quarterly* 58(3): 412–17.

Gilliam, Franklin D., N. A. Valentino, and M. N. Beckmann. 2002. "Where You Live and What You Watch: The Impact of Racial Proximity and Local Television News on Attitudes about Race and Crime." *Political Research Quarterly* 55(4): 755–80.

Glaser, James M. 1994. "Back to the Black Belt: Racial Environment and White Racial Attitudes in the South." *Journal of Politics* 56: 21–41.

Goffman, Erving. 1983. "The Interaction Order." *American Sociological Review* 48: 1–17.

Gordon, Milton M. 1978. *Human Nature, Class and Ethnicity.* New York: Oxford University Press.

———. 1981. "Models of Pluralism: The New American Dilemma." *Annals of the American Academy of Political and Social Sciences* 454: 178–88.

Green, Donald P., Dara Z. Strolovitch, and Janelle S. Wong. 1998. "Defended Neighborhoods, Integration, and Racially Motivated Crime." *American Journal of Sociology* 104: 372–403.

Groves, Robert M., and Mick P. Couper. 1998. *Nonresponse in Household Interview Surveys.* New York: Wiley.

Guterbock, Thomas M., and Bruce London. 1983. "Race, Political Orientation and Participation: An Empirical Test of Four Competing Theories." *American Sociological Review* 48: 439–53.

Hallett, Tim. 2003. "Emotional Feedback and Amplification in Social Interaction." *Sociological Quarterly* 44: 705–26.

Haney-Lopez, Ian. 1996. *White by Law: The Legal Construction of Race.* New York: New York University Press.

Hartigan, John, Jr. 1999. *Racial Situations: Class Predicaments of Whiteness in Detroit.* Princeton, NJ: Princeton University Press.

Hartshorn, Truman A., and Keith R. Ihlanfeldt. 2000. "Growth and Change in Metropolitan Atlanta." In Sjoquist 2000, 15–41.

Hatchett, Shirley J. 1991. "Women and Men" In *Life in Black America*, ed. James Jackson, 84–104. Newbury Park, CA: Sage.

Hawkins, Darnell F. 2001. "Commentary on Randall Kennedy's Overview of the Justice System." In *America Becoming: Racial Trends and Their Consequences, Volume Two*, ed. Neil J. Smelser, William Julius Wilson, and Faith Mitchell, 32–51. Washington, DC: National Academy Press.

Hechter, Michael. 1975. *Internal Colonialism.* Berkeley and Los Angeles: University of California Press.

Henwood, Doug. 1997. "Trash-O-Nomics." In *White Trash: Race and Class in America*, ed. Matt Wray and Annalee Newitz, 177–92. New York: Routledge.

Hewitt, Cynthia M. 2004. "African-American Concentration in Jobs: The Political Economy of Job Segregation and Contestation in Atlanta." *Urban Affairs Review* 39(3): 318–41.

Hirsch, Arnold R. 1995. "Massive Resistance in the Urban North: Trumbull Park, Chicago, 1953–1966." *Journal of American History* 82: 522–50.

Hochschild, Jennifer L. 1995. *Facing Up to the American Dream: Race, Class, and the Soul of the Nation*. Princeton, NJ: Princeton University Press.

Hodson, Randy. 2001. *Dignity at Work*. Cambridge: Cambridge University Press.

Hogan, Dennis P., and David L. Featherman. 1977. "Racial Stratification and Socioeconomic Change in the American North and South." *American Journal of Sociology* 83: 100–126.

Holzer, Harry J. 1996. *What Employers Want: Job Prospects for Less-Educated Workers*. New York: Russell Sage Foundation.

Hout, Michael. 1984. "Occupational Mobility of Black Men: 1962 to 1973." *American Sociological Review* 49: 308–22.

———. 1986. "Opportunity and the Minority Middle-Class: A Comparison of Blacks in the United States and Catholics in Northern Ireland." *American Sociological Review* 51: 214–33.

Hout, Michael, Claude Fischer, Martin Sanchez Jankowski, Samuel R. Lucas, Ann Swidler, and Kim Voss. 1996. *Inequality by Design: Myths, Data, and Politics*. Working Paper 27. Berkeley: University of California, Survey Research Center.

Hughes, Michael, and Melvin E. Thomas. 1998. "The Continuing Significance of Race Revisited: A Study of Race, Class, and Quality of Life in America, 1972 to 1996." *American Sociological Review* 63: 785–95.

Ihlanfeldt, Keith R., and David L. Sjoquist. 2000. "The Geographic Mismatch between Jobs and Housing." In Sjoquist 2000, 116–27.

Ihlanfeldt, Keith R., and Madelyn V. Young. 1994. "Housing Segregation and the Wages and Commutes of Urban Blacks: The Case of Atlanta Fast-Food Restaurant Workers." *Review of Economics and Statistics* (August): 425–33.

Isaacs, Harold. 1961. "A Reporter at Large—Back to Africa." *New Yorker* (May): 135.

Jackman, Mary R. 1994. *The Velvet Glove: Paternalism and Conflict in Gender, Class, and Race Relations*. Berkeley and Los Angeles: University of California Press.

Jackman, Mary R., and Marie Crane. 1986. "Some of My Best Friends Are Black: Interracial Friendships and White Racial Attitudes." *Public Opinion Quarterly* 50(4): 459–86.

Jackman, Mary R., and Michael J. Muha. 1984. "Education and Intergroup Attitudes: Moral Enlightenment, Superficial Democratic Commitment, or Ideological Refinement?" *American Sociological Review* 49: 751–69.

Jacobs, David, and Richard Kleban. 2003. "Political Institutions, Minorities, and Punishment: A Pooled Cross-national Analysis of Imprisonment Rates." *Social Forces* 82(2): 725–55.

Jacobson, Michael Frye. 1998. *Whiteness of a Different Color: European Immigrants and the Alchemy of Race.* Cambridge, MA: Harvard University Press.

Jaret, Charles, Lesley Williams Reid, and Robert M. Adelman. 2003. "Black-White Income Inequality and Metropolitan Socioeconomic Structure." *Journal of Urban Affairs* 25: 305–33.

Jargowsky, Paul A. 1996. "Take the Money and Run: Economic Segregation in U.S. Metropolitan Areas." *American Sociological Review* 61: 984–98.

Jasso, Guillermina. 2001. "Studying Status: An Integrated Framework." *American Sociological Review* 66: 96–124.

Jaynes, Gerald, and Robin Williams. 1989. *A Common Destiny: Blacks and American Society.* Washington, DC: National Academy Press.

Jencks, Christopher. 1992. *Rethinking Social Policy: Race, Poverty, and the Underclass.* Cambridge, MA: Harvard University Press.

Jencks, Christopher, and Susan E. Mayer. 1990. "The Social Consequences of Growing Up in a Poor Neighborhood." In *Inner-City Poverty in the United States,* ed. Laurence E. Lynn Jr. and Michael G. H. McGeary. Washington, DC: National Academy Press.

Johnson, James H., Jr., and Melvin L. Oliver. 1994. "Interethnic Minority Conflict in Urban America: The Effects of Economic and Social Dislocations." In *Race and Ethnic Conflict: Contending Views on Prejudice, Discrimination, and Ethnoviolence,* ed. Fred L. Pincus and Howard J. Ehrlich. Boulder, CO: Westview Press.

Jones, Jacqueline. 1992. *The Dispossessed.* New York: Basic Books.

Kaestner, R., and W. Fleischer. 1992. "Income Inequality as an Indication of Discrimination in Housing Markets." *Review of Black Political Economy* 21: 55–80.

Kalleberg, Arne L., and Larry J. Griffin. 1980. "Class, Occupation, and Inequality in Job Rewards." *American Journal of Sociology* 85(4): 731–68.

Kasinitz, Philip. 1992. *Caribbean New York: Black Immigrants and the Politics of Race.* Ithaca: Cornell University Press.

Kasinitz, Philip, and Jan Rosenberg. 1996. "Missing the Connection: Social Isolation and Employment on the Brooklyn Waterfront." *Social Problems* 43(2): 180–96.

Keating, Larry. 2001. *Atlanta: Race, Class and Urban Expansion*. Philadelphia: Temple University Press.

Kefalas, Maria. 2003. *The Last Garden: Culture and Place in a White Working-Class Chicago Neighborhood*. Berkeley and Los Angeles: University of California Press.

Kelley, Robin D. G. 1994. *Race Rebels: Culture, Politics, and the Black Working Class*. New York: Free Press.

Kennedy, Randall. 2001. "Racial Trends in the Administration of Criminal Justice." In *America Becoming: Racial Trends and Their Consequences, Volume Two*, ed. Neil J. Smelser, William Julius Wilson, and Faith Mitchell, 1–20. Washington, DC: National Academy Press.

Kirchenman, Joleen, and Kathryn Neckerman. 1991. "We'd Love to Hire Them, But . . .": The Meaning of Race for Employers." In *The Urban Underclass*, ed. Christopher Jencks and Paul Peterson, 203–34. Washington, DC: Brookings Institution Press.

Kleinpenning, G., and L. Hagendoorn. 1993. "Forms of Racism and the Cumulative Dimension of Ethnic Attitudes." *Social Psychology Quarterly* 56: 21–36.

Kluegel, James R. 1978. "The Causes and Cost of Racial Exclusion from Job Authority." *American Sociological Review* 43: 285–301.

———. 1990. "Trends in Whites' Explanations of the Black-White Gap in Socioeconomic Status, 1977–1989." *American Sociological Review* 55: 512–25.

Kluegel, James R., and Lawrence D. Bobo. 2001. "Perceived Group Discrimination and Policy Attitudes: The Sources and Consequences of the Race and Gender Gaps." In O'Connor, Tilly, and Bobo 2001, 163–213.

Kluegel, James R. and Eliot R. Smith. 1982. "Whites' Beliefs about Blacks' Opportunity." *American Sociological Review* 47:518–32.

Krysan, Maria. 1998. "Privacy and the Expression of White Racial Attitudes." *Public Opinion Quarterly* 62: 506–44.

———. 1999. "Qualifying a Quantifying Analysis on Racial Equality." *Social Psychology Quarterly* 62: 211–18.

———. 2000. "Prejudice, Politics, and Public Opinion: Understanding the Sources of Racial Policy Attitudes." *Annual Review of Sociology* 26: 135–68.

Lambert, Wallace, and Donald Taylor. 1988. "Assimilation versus Multiculturalism: The Views of Urban Americans." *Sociological Forum* 3: 72–88.

Lamont, Michele. 2000. *The Dignity of Working Men: Morality and the Boundaries of Race, Class, and Immigration*. Cambridge, MA: Harvard University Press.

———, ed. 1999. *The Cultural Territories of Race: Black and White Boundaries*. Chicago: University of Chicago Press.

Lamont, Michele, and Marcel Fournier, eds. 1992. *Cultivating Differences: Symbolic Differences and the Making of Inequality.* Chicago: University of Chicago Press.

Landry, Bart. 1987. *The New Black Middle Class.* Berkeley and Los Angeles: University of California Press.

LaVeist, Thomas A., and Katrina Bell McDonald. 2002. "Race, Gender and Educational Advantage in the Inner City." *Social Science Quarterly* 83(3): 832–52.

Lee, Jennifer. 2000. "The Salience of Race in Everyday Life: Black Customers' Shopping Experiences in Black and White Neighborhoods." *Work and Occupations.* 27: 353–76.

———. 2002. *Civility in the City: Blacks, Jews, and Koreans in Urban America.* Cambridge, MA: Harvard University Press.

Levine, Steven B. 1980. "The Rise of American Boarding Schools and the Development of a National Upper Class." *Social Problems* 28: 63–94.

Lichter, Daniel T. 1989. "Race, Employment Hardship and Inequality in the Nonmetropolitan South." *American Sociological Review* 54: 436–46.

Lieberson, Stanley. 1980. *A Piece of the Pie.* Berkeley and Los Angeles: University of California Press.

Liggett, Robin, Anastasia Loukaitou-Sideris, and Hiroyuki Iseki. 2002. "Journeys to Crime: Assessing the Effects of a Light Rail Line on Crime in the Neighborhoods." Paper presented at the Annual Meeting of the Transportation Research Board, Washington, DC.

Lin, Ann Chih. 1998. "Bridging Positivist and Interpretivist Approaches to Qualitative Methods." *Policy Studies Journal* 26: 162–80.

Lipset, Seymour Martin. 1959. "Democracy and Working-Class Authoritarianism." *American Sociological Review* 24: 482–502.

———. 1981. *Political Man: The Social Bases of Politics.* Baltimore, MD: Johns Hopkins University Press.

Loewen, James W. [1971] 1988. *The Mississippi Chinese.* Cambridge, MA: Harvard University Press. Reprint, Prospect Heights, IL: Waveland.

Logan, John R., and Richard D. Alba. 1993. "Locational Returns to Human Capital." *Demography* 30: 243–68.

Logan, John R., Brian J. Stults, and Reynolds Farley. 2004. "Segregation of Minorities in the Metropolis: Two Decades of Change." *Demography* 41(1): 1–22.

Maines, David R. 2001. *The Faultline of Consciousness: A View of Interactionism in Sociology.* New York: Aldine de Gruyter.

Martin, I., and S. Tuch. 1993. "Black-White Differences in the Value of Job Rewards." *Social Science Quarterly* 74: 884–901.

Massagli, Michael. 2000. "What Do Boston-Area Residents Think of One Another?" In *The Boston Renaissance*, ed. Barry Bluestone and Mary Huff Stevenson, 144–64. New York: Russell Sage Foundation.

Massey, Douglas, and Nancy Denton. 1988. "The Dimensions of Residential Segregation." *Social Forces* 67: 281–315.

———. 1993. *American Apartheid*. Cambridge, MA: Harvard University Press.

Massey, Douglas, and Mitchell L. Eggers. 1990. "The Ecology of Inequality." *American Journal of Sociology* 95: 1153–88.

Massey, Douglas, and Eric Fong. 1990. "Segregation and Neighborhood Quality." *Social Forces* 69: 15–32.

Massey, Douglas S., and Deborah S. Hirst. 1998. "From Escalator to Hourglass: Changes in the U.S. Occupational Wage Structure, 1949–1989." *Social Science Research* 27: 51–71.

Massey, Douglas, and S. Kanaiaupuni. 1993. "Public Housing and the Concentration of Poverty." *Social Science Quarterly* 74: 109–22.

McAdam, Douglas. 1982. *Political Process and the Development of Black Insurgency*. Chicago: University of Chicago Press.

McDermott, Monica. 2002. "Trends in the Race and Ethnicity of Eminent Americans." *Sociological Forum* 17: 137–60.

McGreevy, John T. 1996. *Parish Boundaries: The Catholic Encounter with Race in the Twentieth-Century Urban North*. Chicago: University of Chicago Press.

Memmi, Albert. 2000. *Racism*. Minneapolis: University of Minnesota Press.

Miller, Marc S., ed. 1980. *Working Lives: The Southern Exposure History of Labor in the South*. New York: Pantheon Books.

Mitchell, Richard G. 1993. *Secrecy and Fieldwork*. Newbury Park, CA: Sage Publications.

Morgan, Kathleen O'Leary, and Scott Morgan, eds. 2002. *City Crime Rankings: Crime in Metropolitan America*. Lawrence, KS: Morgan Quitno Press.

Moss, Philip, and Chris Tilly. 2001. *Stories Employers Tell: Race, Skill, and Hiring in America*. New York: Russell Sage Foundation.

Mufuka, K. Nyamayaro. 1997. *Letters from America: An African's View of American Culture*. Harare, Zimbabwe: Anvil Press.

Mullins, Elizabeth I., and Paul Sites. 1984. "The Origins of Contemporary Eminent Black Americans: A Three-Generation Analysis of Social Origin." *American Sociological Review* 49: 672–85.

Murguia, Edward, and Tyrone Forman. 2003. "Shades of Whiteness: The Mexican American Experience in Relation to Anglos and Blacks." In *White Out:*

The Continuing Significance of Racism, ed. Ashley Doane and Eduardo Bonilla-Silva, 63–80. New York: Routledge.

Nagel, Joane. 2003. *Race, Ethnicity, and Sexuality: Intimate Intersections, Forbidden Frontiers*. New York: Oxford University Press.

National Institute for Occupational Safety and Health. 1996. "Violence in the Workplace: Risk Factors and Prevention Strategies." *Current Intelligence Bulletin* 57. Washington, DC: U.S. Department of Health and Human Services.

Newman, Katherine. 1993. *Declining Fortunes: The Withering of the American Dream*. New York: Basic Books.

———. 1999. *No Shame in My Game: The Working Poor in the Inner City*. New York: Knopf; Russell Sage Foundation.

NIOSH. *See* National Institute for Occupational Safety and Health.

O'Connor, Alice, Chris Tilly, and Lawrence D. Bobo, eds. 2001. *Urban Inequality: Evidence from Four Cities*. New York: Russell Sage Foundation.

Office of Management and Budget. 2000. "Standards for Defining Metropolitan and Micropolitan Statistical Areas." *Federal Register* 65(249): 82228–38.

Oliver, J. Eric, and Tali Mendelberg. 2000. "Reconsidering the Environmental Determinants of White Racial Attitudes." *American Journal of Political Science* 44: 574–89.

Oliver, Melvin L., and Thomas M. Shapiro. 1997. *Black Wealth/White Wealth: A New Perspective on Racial Inequality*. New York: Routledge.

Omi, Michael, and Howard Winant. 1986. *Racial Formation in the United States*. New York: Routledge and Kegan Paul.

Orfield, Gary. 2001. *Schools More Separate: Consequences of a Decade of Resegregation*. Cambridge, MA: Harvard Civil Rights Project, Harvard University.

Paquette, Michael J. 2000. "Unity Elusive for African Immigrants." *New Orleans Times-Picayune* (18 June, 2000).

Patterson, Orlando. 1972. "Toward a Future That Has No Past—Reflections on the Fate of Blacks in the Americas." *Public Interest* 27: 25–62.

———. 1989. "Toward a Study of Black America." *Dissent* (Fall): 476–86.

Paules, Greta Foff. *Dishing It Out: Power and Resistance among Waitresses in a New Jersey Restaurant*. Philadelphia: Temple University Press.

Pettigrew, Thomas. 1985. "New Patterns of Racism: The Different Worlds of 1984 and 1964." *Rutgers Law Review* 37(4): 673–705.

———. 2000. "Systematizing the Predictors of Prejudice." In Sears, Sidanius, and Bobo 2000.

Pettigrew, Thomas, and Joanne Martin. 1987. "Shaping the Organizational Context for Black American Inclusion." *Journal of Social Issues* 43(1): 41–78.

Pettigrew, Thomas, and R. W. Meertens. 1995. "Subtle and Blatant Prejudice in Western Europe." *European Journal of Social Psychology* 25: 57–75.

Pinderhughes, Howard. 1993. "The Anatomy of Racially Motivated Violence in New York City: A Case Study of Youth in Southern Brooklyn." *Social Problems* 40(4): 478–92.

Poister, Theodore H. 1996. "Transit-Related Crime in Suburban Areas." *Journal of Urban Affairs* 18(1): 63–75.

Pomer, Marshall I. 1986. "Labor Market Structure, Intragenerational Mobility, and Discrimination: Black Male Advancement Out of Low Paying Occupations, 1962–1973." *American Sociological Review* 51: 650–59.

Quillian, Lincoln. 1996. "Group Threat and Regional Change in Attitudes Towards African-Americans." *American Journal of Sociology* 102: 816–61.

Ridgeway, Cecilia, and Kristan Glasgow Erickson. 2000. "Creating and Spreading Status Beliefs." *American Journal of Sociology* 106: 579–615.

Ridgeway, Cecilia, and Henry A. Walker. 1995. "Status Structures." In *Sociological Perspectives on Social Psychology*, ed. Karen Cook, Gary Alan Fine, and James S. House, 281–310. Boston, MA: Allyn and Bacon.

Rieder, Jonathan. 1985. *Canarsie: The Jews and Italians of Brooklyn against Liberalism*. Cambridge, MA: Harvard University Press.

Rodkin, Philip C. 1993. "The Psychological Reality of Social Constructions." *Ethnic and Racial Studies* 16: 633–56.

Roedemeier, Chad. 2000. "Atlanta Airport is First Stop for African Immigrants Chasing Dreams." *Florida Times-Union* (7 May, 2000).

Roediger, David R. 1991. *The Wages of Whiteness: Race and the Making of the American Working Class*. London: Verso.

Roemer, John E. 1982. *A General Theory of Exploitation and Class*. Cambridge, MA: Harvard University Press.

———. 1982. "New Directions in the Marxian Theory of Exploitation and Class." *Politics and Society* 11(3): 253–87.

Ross, C., and J. Stein. 1985. "Business and Residential Perceptions of a Proposed Rail Station: Implications for Transit Planning." *Transportation Quarterly* 39(4): 483–93.

Ruggles, Steven, Matthew Sobek, Trent Alexander, Catherine A. Fitch, Ronald Goeken, Patricia Kelly Hall, Miriam King, and Chad Ronnander. 2004. *Integrated Public Use Microdata Series, Version 3.0* [Machine-readable database]. Minneapolis: Minnesota Population Center [producer and distributor].

Sampson, Robert J., and William Julius Wilson. 1995. "Toward a Theory of Race, Crime, and Inequality." In *Crime and Inequality*, ed. John Hagan and Ruth Peterson, 37–54. Stanford, CA: Stanford University Press.

Sampson, William A., and Vera Milam. 1975. "The Interracial Attitudes of the Black Middle Class: Have They Changed?" *Social Problems* 23: 153–65.

Schuman, Howard, and Lawrence Bobo. 1988. "Survey-Based Experiments on White Racial Attitudes toward Residential Integration." *American Journal of Sociology* 94: 273–99.

Schuman, Howard, and Stanley Presser. 1981. *Questions and Answers in Attitude Surveys: Experiments on Question Form, Wording and Context.* New York: Academic Press.

Schuman, Howard, Charlotte Steeh, Lawrence Bobo, and Maria Krysan. 1997. *Racial Attitudes in America.* Cambridge, MA: Harvard University Press.

Sears, David O. 1988. "Symbolic Racism." In *Eliminating Racism*, ed. Phyllis A. Katz and Dalmas A. Taylor, 53–84. New York: Plenum.

Sears, David O., John J. Hetts, Jim Sidanius, and Lawrence Bobo. 2000. "Race in American Politics," In Sears, Sidanius, and Bobo 2000.

Sears, David O., Jim Sidanius, and Lawrence Bobo, eds. 2000. *Racialized Politics: The Debate about Racism in America.* Chicago: University of Chicago Press.

Seltzer, Richard, and Robert C. Smith. 1985. "Race and Ideology: A Research Note Measuring Liberalism and Conservatism in Black America." *Phylon* 46: 98–105.

Sennett, Richard, and Jonathan Cobb. 1972. *The Hidden Injuries of Class.* New York: Knopf.

Shanahan, Suzanne, and Susan Olzak. 1999. "The Effects of Immigrant Diversity and Ethnic Competition on Collective Conflict in Urban America: An Assessment of Two Moments of Mass Migration, 1869–1924 and 1965–1993." *Journal of American Ethnic History* 18(3): 30–64.

Sigelman, Lee, and Susan Welch. 1993. "The Contact Hypothesis Revisited: Black-White Interaction and Positive Racial Attitudes." *Social Forces* 71: 781–95.

Sjoquist, David L., ed. 2000. *The Atlanta Paradox.* New York: Russell Sage Foundation.

Skrentny, John David. 1996. *The Ironies of Affirmative Action.* Chicago: University of Chicago Press.

Smith, Joan, ed. 1988. *Racism, Sexism and the World-System.* Westport, CT: Greenwood Press.

Smith, Robert C., and Richard Seltzer. 1992. *Race, Class, and Culture.* Albany: State University of New York Press.

Smith, Sandra S., and Mignon R. Moore. 2000. "Intraracial Diversity and Relations among African-Americans: Closeness among Black Students at a Predominantly White University." *American Journal of Sociology* 106: 1–39.

Sniderman, Paul, and Edward Carmines. 1997. *Reaching Beyond Race.* Cambridge, MA: Harvard University Press.

Sniderman, Paul, and Thomas Piazza. 1993. *The Scar of Race.* Cambridge, MA: Harvard University Press.

Snow, David A. 1999. "Assessing the Ways in Which Qualitative/Ethnographic Research Contributes to Social Psychology: Introduction to the Special Issue." *Social Psychology Quarterly* 62: 97–100.

South, Scott J., and Glenn D. Deane. 1993. "Race and Residential Mobility." *Social Forces* 72: 147–67.

Soysal, Yasemin. 1994. *Limits of Citizenship: Migrants and Postnational Membership in Europe.* Chicago: University of Chicago Press.

Spenner, Kenneth I. 1988. "Social Stratification, Work and Personality." *Annual Review of Sociology* 14: 69–97.

Stafford, Susan Buchanan. 1987. "The Haitians: The Cultural Meaning of Race and Ethnicity." In *New Immigrants in New York*, ed. Nancy Foner, 131–58. New York: Columbia University Press.

Steeh, Charlotte, and Howard Schuman. 1992. "Young White Adults: Did Racial Attitudes Change in the 1980s?" *American Journal of Sociology* 98(2): 340–67.

Storrs, Debbie. 1999. "Whiteness as Stigma: Essentialist Identity Work by Mixed Race Women." *Symbolic Interaction* 22: 187–212.

Sugrue, Thomas. 1996. *The Origins of the Urban Crisis: Race and Inequality in Postwar Detroit.* Princeton, NJ: Princeton University Press.

Suttles, Gerald. 1972. *The Social Construction of Communities.* Chicago: University of Chicago Press.

Swidler, Ann. 1986. "Culture in Action: Symbols and Strategies." *American Sociological Review* 51: 273–86.

Tajfel, Henri. 1978. *Differentiation between Social Groups: Studies in the Social Psychology of Intergroup Relations.* New York: Academic Press.

Taylor, D. Garth. 1979. "Housing, Neighborhoods, and Race Relations: Recent Survey Evidence." *Annals of the American Academy of Political and Social Sciences* 441: 26–40.

Taylor, Marylee. 1998. "The Effect of Racial Composition on Racial Attitudes of Whites." *American Sociological Review* 63: 512–535.

Teixiera, Ruy, and Joel Rogers. 2000. *America's Forgotten Majority: Why the White Working Class Still Matters.* New York: Basic Books.

Thomas, Melvin E. 1993. "Race, Class, and Personal Income: An Empirical Test of the Declining Significance of Race Thesis, 1968–1988." *Social Problems* 40: 328–42.

Thomas, Melvin E., and Michael Hughes. 1986. "The Continuing Significance of Race: A Study of Race, Class, and Quality of Life in America, 1972–1985." *American Sociological Review* 51: 830–41.

Thompson, Mark A. 2000. "Black-White Residential Segregation in Atlanta." In Sjoquist 2000, 88–115.

Tuch, Steven A. 1988. "Race Differences in the Antecedents of Social Distance Attitudes." *Sociology and Social Research* 72(3): 181–84.

Ulmer, J., and M. Wilson. 2003. "The Potential Contributions of Quantitative Research to Symbolic Interactionism." *Symbolic Interaction* 26(4): 531–52.

Warren, Jonathan W., and France Winndance Twine. 1997. "White Americans, The New Minority? Non-Blacks and the Ever-Expanding Boundaries of Whiteness." *Journal of Black Studies* 28: 200–218.

Waters, Mary C. 1990. *Ethnic Options: Choosing Identities in America.* Berkeley and Los Angeles: University of California Press.

———. 1992. "Multiple Ethnic Identities and Identity Choices." Paper presented at the American Pluralism: Toward a History of the Discussion Conference, Stony Brook, NY, June 5–6.

———. 1994. "The Social Construction of Race and Ethnicity: Some Examples from Demography." Paper presented at the Center for Social and Demographic Analysis Conference. Albany, NY, April 15–16.

———. 1999. *Black Identities: West Indian Immigrant Dreams and American Realities.* Cambridge, MA: Harvard University Press.

Weigel, Russell H., and Paul W. Howes. 1985. "Conceptions of Racial Prejudice: Symbolic Racism Reconsidered." *Journal of Social Issues* 41(3): 117–38.

Weisbord, Robert G. 1974. *Ebony Kinship: Africa, Africans, and the Afro-American.* Westport, CT: Greenwood Press.

Wellman, David. [1977] 1993. *Portraits of White Racism.* Reprint, Cambridge: Cambridge University Press.

White, Harrison. 1992. *Identity and Control.* Princeton, NJ: Princeton University Press.

Williams, Richard. 1990. *Hierarchical Structures and Social Value.* Cambridge: Cambridge University Press.

Willie, Charles Vert. 1989. *The Caste and Class Controversy on Race and Poverty.* Dix Hills, NY: General Hall.

Wilson, Jill. 2003. *African-Born Residents of the United States*. Washington, DC: Migration Policy Institute.

Wilson, Thomas C. 1986. "Interregional Migration and Racial Attitudes." *Social Forces* 65(1): 177–86.

Wilson, William Julius. 1973. *Power, Racism and Privilege*. New York: Free Press.

———. 1978. *The Declining Significance of Race*. Chicago: University of Chicago Press.

———. 1987. *The Truly Disadvantaged*. Chicago: University of Chicago Press.

Winant, Howard. 2000. "Race and Race Theory." *Annual Review of Sociology* 26: 169–185.

Wright, Erik Olin. 1978. *Class, Crisis and the State*. London: NLB.

———. 1979. *Class Structure and Income Determination*. New York: Academic Press.

———. 1985. *Classes*. London: Verso.

———. 1994. *Interrogating Inequality*. London: Verso.

Wright, Erik Olin, Andrew Levine, and Elliot Sober. 1992. *Reconstructing Marxism*. London: Verso.

Yancey, George A. 2003. *Who Is White? Latinos, Asians, and the New Black/Nonblack Divide*. Boulder, CO: Lynne Rienner Publishers.

Yinger, John 1995. *Closed Doors, Opportunities Lost: The Continuing Cost of Housing Discrimination*. New York: Russell Sage Foundation.

Zweigenhaft, Richard L., and G. William Domhoff. 1991. *Blacks in the White Establishment*. New Haven, CT: Yale University Press.

Zwerling, Craig, and Hilary Silver. 1992. "Race and Job Dismissals in a Federal Bureaucracy." *American Sociological Review* 57: 651–60.

INDEX

affirmative action programs: white opposition to, 3, 39, 51; white support of, 68

African Americans, use of term, 161–62. *See also* black *entries*

African immigrants, 21; adaptation of, 102–3; in Atlanta, 81–82, 150; black racial identity and, 102; black working-class attitudes toward, 80, 82–88, 161; male cab drivers, 82–83; research on, 82; U.S. destinations of, 165n1; white views of, 150; women, 83

Alba, Richard D., 8

alcohol/alcoholism, as coping mechanism, 111, 129

Allen, Theodore W., 15

Anderson, Elijah, 109, 119, 129, 131

Antoine (black General Fuel worker), 76–77, 108

apologies, as power, 65–66, 78

Apraku, Kofi, 82, 86

Arthur, John A., 82, 86

Asian immigrants, 7, 16–17, 131

Associated Press, 164n4

Atlanta: affirmative action as viewed in, 51; African immigrants in, 81–88, 150; black/black immigrant relations in, 102–3; black criminal stereotype in, 117–24; black housing projects in, 118–20; black middle class in, 23–25; black population of, 19–22, 23 table 3, 25 table 5; black-white interaction in, 2–3; crime in, 74–77, 104, 166n1; demographics of, 19–23, 20 table 1; non-Hispanic white population of, 21, 22 table 2, 24 table 4; political/economic history of, 23–28; poor/working class blacks in, 25; public schools in, 74; public transportation and crime in, 120–22; research site selection in, 12–13, 159–60; residential segregation in, 26–27, 27 table 6; unionization in, 27–28; white-black dissimilarity index in, 164n4. *See also* "Crescent" neighborhood; "General Fuel"

Bayor, Ronald H., 27

Beckmann, M. N., 105

Bellair, Paul, 8

Bennett, Gary G., 60

Bettie, Julie, 43

bisexuality, 133–34, 144

Bixler, Mark, 81

"black, acting," 94–95, 100, 101
black differentiation strategies: with
     African immigrants, 87–88, 161;
     with Haitian immigrants, 92–93;
     with poor blacks, 93–98, 165n8; sol-
     idarity vs., 96–97; white perception
     of, 98–101
black men: as convenience store
     cashiers, 30; criminal stereotype of,
     17, 37, 43, 104–5, 150; gender
     stereotypes and, 146–47; impact of
     racial prejudice on, 59–60;
     imprisonment rates of, 104, 129;
     interracial flirtations and, 140–41;
     "nigga" and, 80, 97; sexual
     stereotypes of, 130–31, 132, 133,
     147; as viewed by black women,
     93–94, 97, 134–35
black middle class: in Atlanta, 23–25;
     black class divisions and, 79;
     research on, 80, 152; sexuality and,
     134; white perception of, 98–99
black neighborhoods, as dangerous,
     122–23, 128
black racial identity, 102–3, 152
blacks: class/ethnic diversity among,
     79–81; criminal stereotype, 112–13,
     117–24; gender segregation and, 7;
     immigrant economic threat and,
     102–3; in interracial marriages, 131;
     racial inequality and, 5–9; racism
     perceived against, 59–60; as respon-
     sible for socioeconomic problems,
     73–74; white racial prejudice as per-
     ceived by, 60–65; white stereotypes
     of, 3
black threat, 76. See also group threat
     perceptions
black-white interaction: at Atlanta site,
     31; at Boston site, 34–35, 51–54;
     conflicting racial attitudes and, 3–4;
     interpersonal relationships, 66–67,
     151–52; misperceptions in, 152,
     155; racial inequality and, 5; racial

prejudice and, 67, 148–49; racism
     perceived in, 59–60, 61, 77–78;
     school desegregation and, 7–8;
     social class and, 12; social distanc-
     ing, 51–54, 66; in South, 1–2, 163n3
     (Intro.); symbolic interactionist
     view of, 13–14; white racial identity
     and, 2–3
black women: black men as viewed by,
     93–94, 97, 134–35; gender norms
     and femininity of, 143–45; interra-
     cial dating as viewed by, 132,
     132–36. See also specific black cashier
black working class: African immigrants
     as viewed by, 82–88; black middle
     class as viewed by, 98–99; differenti-
     ation strategies among, 93–98;
     Haitian immigrants as viewed by,
     88–89; negative behavior of, in
     "Crescent," 47; punitive attitudes of,
     126–27, 129; racial attitudes of, 29,
     80, 81; racism perceived against,
     59–60; research on, 79–80; signifi-
     cance of, 80
Blanche (white Crescent resident), 29
Blank, Rebecca M., 8
Blumer, Herbert, 13–14, 57, 153
Blumstein, Alfred, 8
Bobo, Lawrence, 3, 10–11, 14, 48,
     102, 153
Bonacich, Edna, 10
Boston: affirmative action as viewed in,
     51; antibusing controversy in, 32;
     black/black immigrant relations in,
     102–3; black population of, 21–22,
     23 table 3, 25 table 5, 56; black-
     white interaction in, 2; Caribbean
     immigrants in, 88–93, 150, 165n5;
     class consciousness in, 57; crime rate
     in, 104, 166n1; demographics of,
     19–23, 20 table 1; ethnic conscious-
     ness in, 56; immigrant population
     of, 19, 21; non-Hispanic white pop-
     ulation of, 21, 22 table 2, 24 table 4;

political/economic history of, 31–32; "Quickie Mart" convenience store in, 33–35, 50–51; research site selection in, 12–13, 159–60; residential segregation in, 31–32. *See also* "Greenfield" neighborhood; "Quickie Mart"

Boston Police Department, 125

Boston Public Schools, 32

Bourgois, Philippe, 109, 131

Brookings Institution Center on Urban and Metropolitan Policy, 26

Caribbean immigrants: adaptation of, 102–3; black racial identity and, 102; black working-class attitudes toward, 80, 86; in Boston, 21, 33, 88; child-rearing practices of, 87. *See also* Haitian immigrants

Carmines, Edward, 152–53

Chad (black Quickie Mart customer), 92–93

Charles, Camille Zubrinsky, 6

Chicago, 55, 165n1

civil rights movement, 1, 73–74

class. *See* black working class; social class; white working class

Clovis (white Crescent resident), 1, 73

Cobain, Kurt, 138

Cobb, Jonathan, 154

code-switching, 109

Collins, Randall, 150–51

Collins, Sharon M., 7, 47

Condran, John G., 163n3 (Intro.)

Conley, Dalton, 6–7

convenience stores: crime at, 105, 108, 112–13; customer profiling at, 106, 113, 114; dangers of work at, 107–13, 128, 140–41; employee coping mechanisms at, 107, 108–11, 143; employee theft at, 115; as research sites, 130; theft prevention at, 114–15. *See also* "General Fuel"; "Quickie Mart"

Cotter, David A., 7

Cotton, Jeremiah, 7

counterfeit bills, 114

Crane, Marie, 12

"Crescent" neighborhood (Atlanta), 39; black-white interaction in, 66–67; coping strategies in, 129; crime rate in, 104, 106–7, 128; criminal threat in, 117–20; description of, 28–29; interpersonal relationships in, 151; low-wage hiring practices in, 42–47; police harassment in, 124–25; racial prejudice in, contexts of, 77–78; relationship with Atlanta, 160; research design in, 164n5; residents of, 157; stereotypes of whites in, 41–43, 46–48; trust/suspicion in, 114; whiteness as inferiority in, 40–49, 150; white racial identity in, 56–58; white racial prejudice in, 60; white racial prejudice in, black perceptions of, 60–64. *See also* "General Fuel"; "Holton"

crime: convenience stores as targets of, 105; gender relations and, 147; negative effects of, 106–7; racial prejudice and, 74–77, 104, 112–13, 117–24, 150

criminal justice system: black views of, 126–28, 129; punitivity of, 161–62; racial inequality in, 8, 104–5

criminal profiling, 106, 113, 114, 128–29

culture of poverty, 43

D'Alessio, Stewart J., 105

Dawson, Michael, 79, 152

DeKalb County (Ga.), 121

Delaney, D., 56

Denton, Nancy, 6

Detroit, 49, 55, 57–58

differentiation. *See* black differentiation strategies

Dillingham, Gerald L., 79

disenfranchisement, political, 1

dissimilarity indices, 164nn3–4
Dodoo, F. Nii-Amoo, 81–82
domestic violence, 165n3
Doug (white General Fuel customer):
    author's relationship with, 161; on
    black class divisions, 72–73; on black
    criminal threat, 75, 118–19; white
    crime/violence and, 75–76; white
    racism and, 74
drug abuse, race and, 47–48
Duane (white Quickie Mart worker),
    110–13, 117, 120
Duneier, Mitchell, 163n1 (Pref.)
Durr, Kenneth D., 55

Earl (white Crescent resident), 69, 74
economic competition: racial prejudice
    and, 10–11; white anti-Haitian atti-
    tudes and, 91–92; white working
    class and, 4–5
Edgar, Walter, 52
education: African immigrants and,
    81–82; impact on wages, 5; racial
    inequality in, 7–8; racial prejudice
    and, 10–11, 74, 150; residential seg-
    regation and, 6; social class and, 16
Ehrenreich, Barbara, 154
Eitle, David, 8, 105
Eitle, Tamela McNulty, 8
Ellen, Ingrid Gould, 6
Ellison, Christopher G., 9, 10
employment: African immigrants and,
    81; residential segregation and, 6.
    See also low-wage employment
Enrico (black General Fuel customer), 108
Eritrean immigrants, 81
Ethiopian immigrants, 81
ethnic consciousness, white racial iden-
    tity and, 55, 56
ethnosexual boundaries, 130–31
European immigrants, 19

Farley, Reynolds, 6
Feagin, Joe R., 7, 79

femininity, sexual orientation and,
    143–47
Fielding, Elaine L., 6
Fine, Gary Alan, 6
Finlay, Nikki McIntyre, 44
flirtations, male-female, 139–43
food stamps, 165n6
Forman, Tyrone, 5
Formisano, Ronald P., 32, 55
Fossett, Mark A., 10
Franklin, Raymond S., 60
Freaknik (Atlanta festival), 123–24
Fulton County (Ga.): crime rate in,
    104; racial composition of, 27
    table 6
Fulton Mills strike (1914–15), 28
fundamentalism, religious, racial atti-
    tudes and, 9–10

gender: black differentiation strategies
    and, 97; crime and, 77; criminal pro-
    filing and, 106; dominant norms, and
    femininity, 143–47; race and, 130–32
gender segregation, 7
"General Fuel" (Atlanta research site):
    author hired at, 45; crime at, 108;
    crime prevention measures at, 105,
    107; criminal threat at, 117–18,
    123–24; customer profiling at, 106,
    114; description of, 29–31; dress code
    at, 145; employee coping mechanisms
    at, 107, 108–10; gender norms and
    femininity at, 143–45; male-female
    flirtations at, 139–40, 141–43;
    personnel/customers at, 157; race and
    sexuality at, 130, 131, 132–36, 137–39;
    research methodology in, 160–62
Georgia, unionization in, 164n1 (Ch. 1)
Ghanaian immigrants, 81
"ghetto": black criminal threat and,
    118–20; black differentiation strate-
    gies and, 93–96, 100–101; black use
    of, 80, 84–85; as coping mechanism,
    109–10, 129

Gilliam, Franklin D., 105
Goffman, Erving, 13, 14–15
Green, Donald P., 55
"Greenfield" neighborhood (Boston):
    black-white interaction in, 66–67;
    coping strategies in, 129; crime rate
    in, 104, 106–7, 128; criminal threat
    in, 120; description of, 32–33;
    Haitian immigrants in, 165n5; inter-
    personal relationships in, 151; police
    racial attitudes in, 125–26; racial
    prejudice in, contexts of, 77–78;
    relationship with Boston, 160;
    research design in, 164n5; residents
    of, 158; social distancing in, 51–54;
    trust/suspicion in, 114; whiteness as
    inferiority in, 40–41; whiteness as
    privilege in, 49–54, 149–50; white
    racial identity in, 56–58; white racial
    prejudice in, 60; white racial preju-
    dice in, black perceptions of, 64–65.
    See also "Quickie Mart"
Greg (white Crescent resident), 124
group threat perceptions: gender rela-
    tions and, 147; immigration and,
    90–91, 101–3; imprisonment rates
    and, 104–5; public transportation
    and, 120–22; race and, 11, 114,
    117–24, 150; research on, 153; white
    racial identity and, 153
Gus (white Quickie Mart manager):
    anti-Haitian attitudes of, 90, 91–92;
    author hired by, 50–51; author's
    relationship with, 161; black immi-
    grant customers and, 64–65; black
    threat and, 76; crime prevention
    measures of, 112, 115–16; interracial
    dating as viewed by, 136–37; racial
    prejudice of, 54, 92

Haitian immigrants: American black atti-
    tudes toward, 88–89; American blacks
    as viewed by, 88–89; black immigrant
    attitudes toward, 92–93; black racial

identity and, 102; in Boston, 22;
    child-rearing practices of, 165n4;
    poor English skills of, 90, 92, 165n5;
    white attitudes toward, 89–92, 150
Hallett, Tim, 60
Hank (white General Fuel owner):
    author hired by, 45; black threat
    and, 123; crime prevention measures
    of, 105, 107; racial attitudes of, 72,
    76–77; white Crescent residents as
    viewed by, 46
Hartigan, John, Jr., 38, 57–58
Hartshorn, Truman A., 26
Harvey (white General Fuel worker),
    70, 117–18
Hawkins, Darnell F., 8
Henwood, Doug, 5
Hermsen, Joan M., 7
Hewitt, Cynthia M., 28
"Hillbillies," 49
Hirsch, Arnold R., 55
Hirst, Deborah S., 5
Hispanics, 7, 16–17
Hochschild, Jennifer L., 7, 79, 152
"Holton" (Ga.): description of, 28–29;
    police harassment in, 124–25; racial
    prejudice in, 68–69; white violence
    in, 75–76; white working class in,
    46, 149. *See also* "Crescent" neigh-
    borhood (Atlanta)
home ownership, 6–7, 53–54
housing policies, racial discrimination
    in, 6
Houston (Tex.), 165n1
Howes, Paul W., 11
humor: as coping mechanism, 108, 129;
    in interracial flirtations, 136–37
Hutchings, Vincent L., 10–11

Ihlanfeldt, Keith R., 26
immigration, race and, 101–3. *See also*
    African immigrants; Caribbean
    immigrants; Haitian immigrants;
    specific immigrant group

imprisonment: black views of, 126–28, 129; rates, 104–5
income inequality, 7
individualism, 43
interaction, face-to-face, 14–15. *See also* black-white interaction
intermarriage, 3, 131
Invisible Sojourners (Arthur), 82
Irish immigrants, 19, 22, 33, 102, 164n1 (Ch. 2)
Isaacs, Harold, 82
Iseki, Hiroyuki, 121
Italian immigrants, 19, 22

Jackman, Mary R., 11–12
Jacobs, David, 104
Jacobson, Michael Frye, 102
Jamaican immigrants, 88, 150, 165n5
Jan (black General Fuel worker), 133–34, 135, 144
Jerry (white Crescent resident), 29, 66–67, 69, 124–25
Jewish immigrants, 102
Jimmy (white Quickie Mart customer), 91
John (white Quickie Mart customer), 65–66, 161
Joyce (white General Fuel customer), 74

Kasinitz, Philip, 6, 79
Katoyah (black General Fuel worker), 64, 138
Keating, Larry, 27
Kefalas, Maria, 55
Kelley, Robin D. G., 79
Kennedy, Randall, 8
Kiecolt, K. Jill, 10
Kim (black General Fuel worker): black criminal threat and, 120; coping strategies of, 95–96, 99, 109–10; ghetto terminology used by, 95–96; interracial dating as viewed by, 135–36
Kirschenman, Joleen, 6

Kleban, Richard, 104
Kluegel, James R., 48
Krysan, Maria, 6

labor market: whiteness as liability in, 38–40, 42–47; whiteness as privilege in, 50–51. *See also* low-wage employment
labor unions: Georgia vs. Massachusetts, 27–28, 164n1 (Ch. 1); white racial identity and, 55, 57
Lambert, Wallace, 4
Lamont, Michele, 41, 55, 148
Landry, Bart, 79
Lashawn (black General Fuel worker), 76–77
Lee, Jennifer, 59, 113, 148
lesbianism, 135–36, 144
Liberian immigrants, 81
Liggett, Robin, 121
Lipset, Seymour Martin, 10
Lisa (white Quickie Mart customer), 117
Logan, John R., 8
Los Angeles, 121, 148
Loukaitou-Sideris, Anastasia, 121
low-wage employment: employee sacrifices for, 110–11; whiteness as liability in, 38–40, 42–47; whiteness as privilege in, 50–51. *See also* convenience stores

Madge (black General Fuel worker): anti-African attitudes of, 83–84, 85–87; author's relationship with, 160–61; black criminal threat and, 120; differentiation strategies of, 94, 95–96, 100–101; gender norms and, 145; on imprisonment, 127; interracial dating as viewed by, 134–35, 137, 138; white working class as viewed by, 42
Manney, Bill, 1
manufacturing sector, decline of, 5
MARTA (Metropolitan Atlanta Rapid Transit Authority), 120–22

Massachusetts, unionization in, 164n1
(Ch. 1)
Massey, Douglas S., 5, 6
MBTA (Metropolitan Boston Transit
Authority), 121
McDermott, Monica, 7
McGreevy, John T., 7
media, black criminal threat and, 105
Memmi, Albert, 15
Metropolitan Atlanta Rapid Transit
Authority (MARTA), 120–22
Metropolitan Boston Transit Authority
(MBTA), 121
metropolitan statistical areas (MSAs),
164n2
Mexican immigrants, 21
Midwest, residential segregation in, 6
Mike (white barber), 67
Miller, Marc S., 57
Million Woman March (Washington,
D.C.), 145
Milt (white Quickie Mart customer),
92–93
Minneapolis, 165n1
Molina (black General Fuel worker):
anti-African attitudes of, 84; author's
relationship with, 160–61; black crim-
inal threat and, 122–23, 128; coping
strategies of, 108, 109; differentiation
strategies of, 94, 95, 96–98; sexual
preferences of, 141–43; white racial
prejudice as perceived by, 61–63
muggings, 75
Multi-City Survey of Urban
Inequality, 102
Mumford Center for Comparative
Urban Research (SUNY at Albany),
27, 164n3
Murguia, Edward, 5
Musick, Marc A., 9, 10

Nagel, Joane, 130–31
National Institute for Occupational
Safety and Health (NIOSH), 105

Neckerman, Kathryn, 6
neighborhood social problems: racial
prejudice and, 60, 74–77
New Jersey, 55
Newman, Katherine, 43
New York, 55, 59, 165n1
Nickel and Dimed (Ehrenreich), 154
Nigerian immigrants, 81
"nigger"/"nigga": black differentiation
strategies and, 97–98, 100, 101;
black use of, 80; white confusion
over, 97
NIOSH, 105
Northeast, 6, 9

Oliver, Melvin L., 6–7
Olzak, Susan, 56
Omi, Michael, 15
Orfield, Gary, 8

participant observation research, 131,
152–53, 159–62
Paules, Greta Foff, 140
Philadelphia, 59, 109
Piazza, Thomas, 152–53
Pinderhughes, Howard, 11
Poister, Theodore H., 121
police: black contempt/mistrust for,
126; black criminal stereotype and,
125–26; brutality, 71; harassment by,
124–25; male-female flirtations and,
141; sexism of, 143
Portuguese immigrants, 19, 164n1 (Ch. 2)
Puerto Rican immigrants, 88, 117, 165n5

"Quickie Mart" (Boston research site):
author hired at, 50–51; crime at,
108, 110–13, 114; crime prevention
measures at, 34, 105, 112, 140; customer profiling at, 106; description
of, 33–35; dress code lacking at, 145;
gender norms and femininity at,
145–47; male-female flirtations at,
139, 140–41; personnel/customers

Quickie Mart (*continued*)
at, 158; race and sexuality at, 130, 131, 136–37; research methodology in, 160–62; violence at, 117
Quillian, Lincoln, 14, 153

race: definition of, 15–16; gender and, 130–32; group threat perception and, 114, 117–24; immigration and, 101–3; politically charged nature of, 4; research methods, 148–49; sexual attractiveness and, 132–39, 150; in working-class communities, 154–55
race/class interaction, 2, 150, 154–55
racial inequality, 5–9, 104–5
racial prejudice, 9–12; black, white perceptions of, 61, 65–66, 78; black discrimination claims as cause of, 68, 70–74; coexistence with cordial interaction, 148–49; contexts of expression, 60, 68–78, 149–50, 153–54; crime and, 104, 112–13, 150; "free-floating," 147, 151; gender relations and, 147; interpersonal relationships and, 67, 151–52; neighborhood social problems as cause of, 74–77; perceptions of, 59–60, 77–78, 152; politically principled, 153; regional differences and, 9–10; social class and, 10–12; in South, 1–2; symbolic interactionist view of, 14; white, black perceptions of, 60–65; white defensiveness as cause of, 68–70
racism, 50, 57; overt, 148
research study: Atlanta site, 28–31; Boston site, 32–35; boundaries of, 16–17; definitions, 15–16; design of, 12–15, 130, 164n5; methods, 35–37, 150–51, 152–53, 159–62
"reverse discrimination," 39, 49
Rieder, Jonathan, 55
robberies, 112
Roedemeier, Chad, 81
Roediger, David R., 15

Rogers, Joel, 80
Rosenberg, Jan, 6
Ross, C., 120
rudeness, 59–60, 63, 162
Rufina (black General Fuel worker), 126–27

Sally (white Crescent employee), 121–22
Sam (white crack dealer), 119
Sampson, Robert J., 8
school desegregation, 7–8, 32, 52–53
Schuman, Howard, 9, 10, 11, 148
segregation, residential: in Atlanta, 26–27, 27 table 6; in Boston, 31–32; decreasing rates of, 3; persistence of, 148; racial inequality and, 6–7
Sennett, Richard, 154
service sector, rise of, 5
sexism, 143
sexuality: black differentiation strategies and, 93; male-female flirtations, 139–43; race and, 130, 132–39, 150; of thugs, 141–42
sexual orientation, feminity and, 143–47
Shanahan, Suzanne, 56
Shapiro, Thomas M., 6–7
Sharon (white Atlanta secretary), 70–71, 143
Sheree (black General Fuel worker): differentiation strategies of, 87–88; gender norms and femininity of, 145; "ghetto" and, 95–96, 100–101, 120
shoplifting, 75, 105, 114, 160
Sikes, Melvin T., 7, 79
Sjoquist, David L., 26
Sniderman, Paul, 152–53
social class: blacks and, 79–81, 101; black socioeconomic problems and, 73–74; definition of, 16; group threat perceptions and, 150; hidden injuries of, 154–55; polarization, 57–58; racial attitudes and, 10–12;

white racial identity and, 53–54, 57.
See also black working class; white
working class
social distancing, 51–54, 66
Somalian immigrants, 81
South: black migration from, 6; black-
white interaction in, 1–2, 163n3
(Intro.); racial prejudice in, 9–10;
unionization in, 57
South Boston, 32
South Carolina, 104–5
Stafford, Susan Buchanan, 86
Steeh, Charlotte, 9, 10, 11
Stein, J., 120
Stephanie (white General Fuel assistant
manager): as "acting black," 94–95;
African immigrant behavior and, 87;
author's relationship with, 160–61;
black threat and, 76, 123–24; interra-
cial dating as viewed by, 133–34, 136;
male-female flirtations with, 141;
sexual preferences of, 141–42; white
Crescent residents as viewed by, 46–47;
on white crime and racism, 71–72
Steve (white Crescent resident), 118–19
Stoltzenberg, Lisa, 105
Storrs, Debbie, 49
"street culture," as coping mechanism,
108–10
Strolovitch, Dara Z., 55
Sugrue, Thomas, 55
Suttles, Gerald, 55
symbolic interactionism, 13–15

Taylor, Donald, 4
Taylor, Marylee, 153
teenagers, male, criminal profiling and,
106, 113, 115–16, 128–29
Teixeira, Ruy, 80
Telika (black General Fuel worker), 83;
anti-African attitudes of, 84–85,
85–87; black criminal threat and,
128; differentiation strategies of, 94,
95, 97, 100–101; gender norms and,
145; on imprisonment, 127–28;

interracial dating as viewed by, 137,
138–39; sexual preferences of,
141–43; white male flirtations with,
138–40; white racial prejudice as
perceived by, 63; white working
class as viewed by, 42
Terry (white Greenfield policeman),
125–26
Tina (black General Fuel worker),
87–88, 110, 165n3
tokenism, 151–52
Tonya (white Quickie Mart worker),
137; black immigrant customers
and, 64–65, 92; gender norms and
femininity of, 145–46; male-female
flirtations with, 140–41
toughness: as coping mechanism, 143,
162; gender norms and, 143–45, 147
Turner, Margery Ellen, 6
Turner, Patricia A., 6
Twine, France Winddance, 55

Ulmer, J., 13
"underclass," 79–80
unemployment, 27
United States: racial divide in, 3, 48, 55;
white racial identity in, 54–56
U.S. Bureau of Labor Statistics, 105,
164n1 (Ch. 1)
U.S. census (1990), 12, 16
U.S. census (2000), 19, 81
U.S. Office of Management and
Budget, 164n2

Valentino, N. A., 105
vandalism, 105
Vanneman, Reeve, 7
violence: black differentiation strategies
and, 93; as coping mechanism,
109–10; domestic, 165n3; negative
effects of, 106–7; race and, 150

Warren, Jonathan W., 55
Washington (D.C.), 165n1
Waters, Mary C., 79, 86, 87

Weigel, Russell H., 11
Weisbord, Robert G., 86
welfare programs, 165n6; white
    opposition to, 10–11, 70, 72
Wellman, David, 10
White, Harrison, 58
white crime/violence, 75–76,
    119, 128
"white flight," 6
white men: black female views of, 133,
    138–39; black women as viewed by,
    137–38
whiteness studies, 56
white racial identity: ambiguous
    function of, 38–40; American racial
    hierarchy and, 55; black-white
    interaction and, 2–3; European
    identification, 19; group threat
    perceptions and, 153; as inferiority,
    40–49, 149; as patterned experience,
    56–58; as privilege, 49–56, 149–50;
    race/class interaction and, 53–54;
    research on, 152
whites: black class divisions and, 79,
    80–81; black differentiation strate-
    gies as viewed by, 98–101; gender
    segregation and, 7; in interracial
    marriages, 131; media and punitive
    attitudes of, 105

white women: interracial dating as
    viewed by, 132; as viewed by black
    lesbians, 135–36
white working class: anti-Haitian atti-
    tudes of, 89–92; Boston antibusing
    controversy and, 32; crime and,
    75–76; economic decline of, 5;
    hidden injuries of class and, 154–55;
    low-wage hiring practices and,
    42–47; negative stereotypes of,
    41–43, 46–48, 67; racial attitudes of,
    4–5, 10–12; white skin privilege and,
    38–40, 55–56, 149–50
Wilson, Jill, 81
Wilson, M., 13
Wilson, Thomas C., 9
Wilson, William Julius, 6, 8
Winant, Howard, 15
women. *See* black women; gender;
    white women
Wong, Janelle S., 55
working-class communities, race in,
    154–55. *See also* black working class;
    white working class
Wright, Erik Olin, 16

Yancey, George A., 10
Yinger, John, 6
Young, Madelyn V., 26

Text: 10/15 Janson

Display: Janson

Compositor: International Typesetting and Composition

Printer and binder: Maple-Vail Manufacturing Group

Indexer: Kevin Millham